School of VISUAL ARTS

Gold:

497

Fifty Years of Creative Graphic Design

For Students, Alumni, Faculty

now—and through the years.

Distributor to the book trade in the United States and Canada
Rizzoli International Publications
through St. Martin's Press
175 Fifth Avenue
New York, NY 10010

Distributor to the art trade in the United States and Canada
PBC International, Inc.
One School Street
Glen Cove, NY 11542

Distributor throughout the rest of the world
Hearst Books International
1350 Avenue of the Americas
New York, NY 10019

Library of Congress Cataloging–in–Publication Data

School of Visual Arts gold : fifty years of creative graphic design /
    School of Visual Arts.
        p. cm.
    Includes index.
    ISBN 0-86636-337-8 (hardcover : alk. paper).
    1. Commercial art--Study and teaching--United States. 2. Graphic
arts--Study and teaching--United States. 3. School of Visual Arts
(New York, N.Y.)--Curricula.   I. School of Visual Arts (New York,
N.Y.)
NC1000.S35 1997
741.6'071'173--dc20   97-20306
                                                      CIP

CAVEAT– Information in this text is believed accurate, and will pose no
problem for the student or casual reader. However, the author was often
constrained by information contained in signed release forms, information
that could have been in error or not included at all. Any misinformation
(or lack of information) is the result of failure in these attestations. The
author has done whatever is possible to insure accuracy.

Color separation by Fine Arts Repro House, Hong Kong
Printing and binding by Dai Nippon Group

10 9 8 7 6 5 4 3 2 1

Printed in Hong Kong

School of VISUAL ARTS
a college of the arts

contents

T H E   W O R K

I N T E R V I E W S

Letter from a Former Student

When I was a freshman in high school in the mid-1960s, every weekday I took the Twenty-third Street cross-town bus to Eighth Avenue where I'd catch a noisy subway that transported me to a prep school on the Upper West Side. Twice a day, coming and going, I passed the former NYU dental college recently turned art school located on Twenty-third Street between Second and Third Avenues where I enviously watched as crowds of long-haired art students wearing army and navy surplus blue peacoats and carrying large black portfolios mingled with their female compatriots before going to class. For the rest of the ride I daydreamed about being one of them—wearing a peacoat, carrying a portfolio, studying art, and generally being released from what seemed like an interminable four-year sentence at hard labor at a conservative boys academy where such appearance, accouterments, and even the study of art was rejected in the pursuit of an Ivy League education. Nevertheless, I was determined to attend that art school, and although I was still years away from even the possibility of enrolling, I kept the dream alive through one of the school's early subway posters that had fortuitously come into my possession.

The poster by George Tscherny, which hung in my room for three years, showed a plaster cast of an ear with a real 2B pencil stuck behind it. At the bottom, in handwritten script was scrawled "School of Visual Arts"; and below that, a discrete line of typeset text read: "Advertising Design, Illustration, Fashion, Cartooning, Audio-Visual Art, Technical and Industrial Art, Fine Arts." I had little inkling as to what all this meant (except for cartooning). But I was so taken with the simplicity and eloquence of this poster that I intuited that this was the essence of a special kind of art, not the musty stuff that hung on museum walls. I continued to be touched by the school's various subway posters by artists whose signatures became increasingly more familiar—Robert Weaver, Bob Gill, Ivan Chermayeff, Milton Glaser, among them. During those years, there were many iconic images hanging in the subway, such as posters for "You Don't Have to Be Jewish to Love Levy's," "Aqueduct Race Track," and "The Urban Coalition," but none grabbed me more for their artistry, intelligence, and wit than the seasonal advertisements celebrating the School of Visual Arts.

As often happens, lives turn, paths twist, and although I had become an obsessive cartoonist, upon graduating from high school I enrolled in NYU as an English major. But I had not lost interest in The School of Visual Arts. In fact, I put myself on the mailing list and regularly received the school catalogs and announcements with the intention of one day taking some additional courses. Then fate interceded; I received a piece of mail that, somehow, forever changed my life. It was a publication edited and designed by students of a magazine course taught by Milton Glaser and Henry Wolf, which was, without a doubt, the most exciting collection of pages I had ever seen. At that time, I was already working as a "layout person" for an underground newspaper, and had been cutting an excessive number of classes to get this work done. So it was this SVA publication with its distinctive typography, unconventional imagery, and cinematic pacing that convinced me that I was wasting my time at NYU. A few months later, I finally enrolled in SVA.

Yet, owing to a personal preoccupation, my academic and attendance record did not, shall we say, make the school proud, and I was eventually and rightfully removed from its rolls. Nevertheless, I consider myself a School of Visual Arts alumnus because I was totally influenced by the school's remarkable graphics. The publications like the one from Glaser and Wolf's class, as well as countless recruitment, exhibition, and lecture posters, and catalogs and booklets had a profound impact on me as an art director and designer—and indeed it had to have had the same effect on anyone who appreciates the strength of images and words in a well composed concert. SVA's print material has served to show how design, illustration, and photography based on ideas, not ethereal trends and fleeting fashions, is the backbone of memorable communications. Without relying on the constraint, or ease, of a "house style," SVA's graphics are diverse, yet distinctly identifiable as emanating from the school. At a time when many art schools succumb to the various new waves, SVA has followed its own—and its contributing artists' and designers' own—visions. SVA's ephemera is not only the historical manifestation of a venerable fifty-year-old institution, it is evidence that the whole can be the sum of its distinctive parts and still be a total entity.

The amazing thing about the past fifty years of The School of Visual Arts' graphic achievement is that those early works are, without exaggeration, as fresh today as they were when they were first conceived; moreover, the work done today is totally consistent with that legacy. Despite changes in the profession, marketplace, and technology, that wonderful "ear" poster which once hung on my wall still conveys its message with clarity and eloquence. As an example of The School of Visual Arts' visual excellence, that is high praise indeed.

Steven Heller

Steven Heller, a senior art director of *The New York Times* and editor of the *AIGA Journal of Graphic Design*, has taught in the School of Visual Arts MFA/Illustration program for ten years and has directed SVA's symposium, "Modernism and Eclecticism: A History of Graphic Design" for nine years.

Silas H. Rhodes (Right) with artist Jerry Moriarty (Left)

this book is about the campus graphics produced over the past fifty years by the School of Visual Arts. Arguably, SVA reinvented the term that is used to describe a variety of promotional and educational material produced by and for universities, colleges and independent art schools.

On the pages that follow, the multipurpose images reflect the singular mission of SVA. It is heartening, also, to observe how these images remain free of the silly and the vulgar—communication without cliches—instructive and entertaining, witty and serious, sometimes profound, never pontifical.

None of the restrictions against using the untried apply to SVA's principles of design. Aesthetics is not sacrificed to communication. On the contrary, the dualism that exists in the commercial world between aesthetics and the need to achieve immediate universal recognition is here resolved.

All the unnecessary distractions and complications of commercialism are stripped away and the standardization of popular art, which so often is merely a synonym for forms that have become stereotyped, never appears.

In its campus graphics, SVA has seized the opportunity and accepted the responsibility to replace the formlessness of arrant commercialism with new forms and new styles drawn from contemporary sources of popular culture—film, theater, literature, architecture, technology and sports.

The zeal for work and the joy of creative endeavor resonate throughout these pages.

SILAS H. RHODES

THE fifties

the decade

of the fifties was a decisive one for the School of Visual Arts. Begun in 1947 as The Cartoonists and Illustrators School, the institution—with its new name adopted in 1956—was ready to forge a new future. It left behind its early antecedents as a single-purpose trade school to teach advertising, cartooning and illustration. And it quickly moved forward to seed intellectual and aesthetic depth to its curriculum and a more "contemporary profession-alism" by adding faculty and staff aligned with its ambitious goals. Visual Arts petitioned the State Department of Education for certification as a three-year, non-degree granting institution in higher education, laying the groundwork for what would become the largest independent art college in the country. The optimism and energy necessary for the School's expansion were reflected in the broader society.

The 1950's was a decade of unprecedented prosperity for America. We were producing half the goods and services in the whole world. Almost 50 million cars were on the road in the U.S. Clearly, "what was good for our country was good for General Motors and vice versa." Corporate America began flexing its power. Advertising became a respectable profession. Television came to stay during the fifties. Nearly one-half of all households had a TV set and it would change forever the way we communicate and the way we think. Personal income doubled by the decade's end and even though history would later characterize this time as one of "empty materialism, complacency and irresponsibility," most Americans were content with their lives and optimistic about the future.

The Korean War and Joseph McCarthy's obsessive witch hunt for communists, the first acknowledgment of global warming, the undercurrent of growing racial inequality all happened in the fifties—events and trends that would continue to influence our American values. And then, too, technological advancements would make air travel accessible to everyone and we would see for ourselves that people, whose customs, lifestyles and standard of living were different from ours, share the planet with us. All in all, this was a decade of learning for Americans. More young men and women were getting advanced educations. And what we learned then would prepare us for more complicated times to come. We began to achieve a visual sophistication, a growing appreciation of the arts, and our confidence soared. The decade in which Rosa Parks refused to give her bus seat to a white man and brought Martin Luther King Jr. to his destiny as a leader and teacher also introduced to the world rock 'n' roll, with its roots in black rhythm and blues. Classic abstract expressionism initiated in the mid-forties—color field and gestural painting—by the fifties was called "the triumph of American painting." American artists like Jackson Pollack, Willem de Kooning and Mark Rothko were elevated to international icons. The accomplishments of the decade were wholly compatible with the American character and the direction in which we were headed.

SUBWAY POSTER *Art Director:* Silas H. Rhodes, *Designer:* George Tscherny

SUBWAY POSTER *Art Director:* Silas H. Rhodes, *Designer:* Ivan Chermayeff

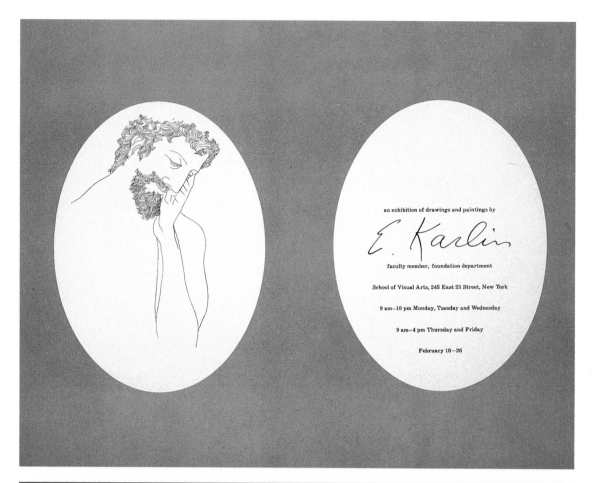

EXHIBIT ANNOUNCEMENTS (Top) *Illustrator:* Eugene Karlin (Bottom) *Illustrator:* Robert Weaver

P H I L   H A Y S

" Early in the fifties, the subways only had hard-core product advertising
and Broadway show promotion—none of it very high quality.
When Silas came up with the poster format for Visual Arts he really introduced
art into the subways. Not since Cassandra in the thirties did posters
have that kind of impact on the public. It was a genius idea.
Before that time posters in general had gone into a real decline. "

A former faculty member at Visual Arts, Phil Hays is now the Chairman of the Illustration Department at The Art Center College of Design in Pasadena, California. Although no longer active as a working illustrator, he continues to teach and now "gets the same satisfaction from my students' art," as he did from doing his own.

WAS THE IMAGE YOU CREATED FOR THIS POSTER TYPICAL OF YOUR WORK AT THE TIME?
Actually, that poster represents a breakthrough period for me. When I came to New York, people loved what I was doing—lots of boy-girl, romantic teenage stuff for *Seventeen*—so I got a lot of that kind of work. But what I really wanted to do was get out of that genre. The poster had a harsher edge to it. The background was very scumbled—a combination of charcoal and watercolor. Very rough and dark. The type was also very important to that poster. John McClash and I worked on it together. When I look at it today, I see a definite Glaser influence on the typography. As for the rest, my influences were Richard Lindner, Andy Warhol, Charles DeMuth and Ben Shahn.

DID ILLUSTRATORS THINK THAT DOING A POSTER FOR VISUAL ARTS BACK THEN WAS IMPORTANT FOR THEIR CAREERS?
It was extremely prestigious, and for me a labor of love. You see, Silas had created an aura around teaching at Visual Arts—if you were anybody, you would be teaching there. And the same went for doing posters. It was a status thing. The posters received tremendous exposure and we all got a lot of work from them. What I remember is that my poster was received really well by the illustrators and other people I most wanted to impress. I rank the ongoing SVA poster campaign equal to the famous Container Corporation of America series. I think it's one of the most important advertising campaigns ever done.

SUBWAY POSTER *Art Director:* Silas H. Rhodes, *Designer:* John McClash, *Illustrator:* Phil Hays

EXHIBIT ANNOUNCEMENT *Art Director:* Silas H. Rhodes, *Designer:* George Tscherny

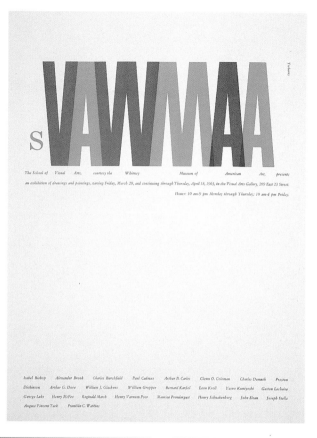

EXHIBIT ANNOUNCEMENTS *Art Director:* George Tscherny

AN EXHIBITION OF THE DESIGN AND ILLUSTRATION OF BOB GILL

AT THE SCHOOL OF VISUAL ARTS, 245 EAST 23RD STREET · APRIL 14 - MAY, 9 1958.
GALLERY HOURS: MON.-THUR. 9 A.M.-10 P.M; FRI. 9 A.M.-4 P.M.
PREVIEW WEDNESDAY APRIL 9, 5-7 P.M.

MR. GILL IS A MEMBER OF THE FACULTY IN THE DEPARTMENT OF DESIGN.

EXHIBIT ANNOUNCEMENT *Illustrator:* Bob Gill

Design: George Tscherny

Head, Foundation Department

John Cabore, his experimental work in fashion drawing and illustration on view at the School of Visual Arts

215 East 23 Street, New York 10, N.Y.

February 16 through March 4, 1959

10 am – 9 pm, Monday, Tuesday, Wednesday, Thursday; 10 am – 3 pm, Friday

EXHIBIT ANNOUNCEMENT *Art Director:* Silas H. Rhodes, *Designer:* George Tscherny

FALL SESSION   begins September 16, 1957   REGISTER NOW

Advertising Design	Magazine Illustration	Layout
Decorative Illustration	Book Illustration	Rendering
Silk Screen	TV Art	Lettering
Package Design	Painting	Typography
Pasteup & Mechanicals	Life Drawing	Airbrush
Cartooning	Stylized Cartooning	Drafting
Anatomy	Graphics	Production
Photo Retouching	Technical Illustration	

SCHOOL of VISUAL ARTS

245 EAST 23rd STREET   NEW YORK 10   MUrray Hill 3-8397

Licensed by the State of New York

SUBWAY POSTER *Art Director:* Silas H. Rhodes, *Illustrator:* Eugene Karlin

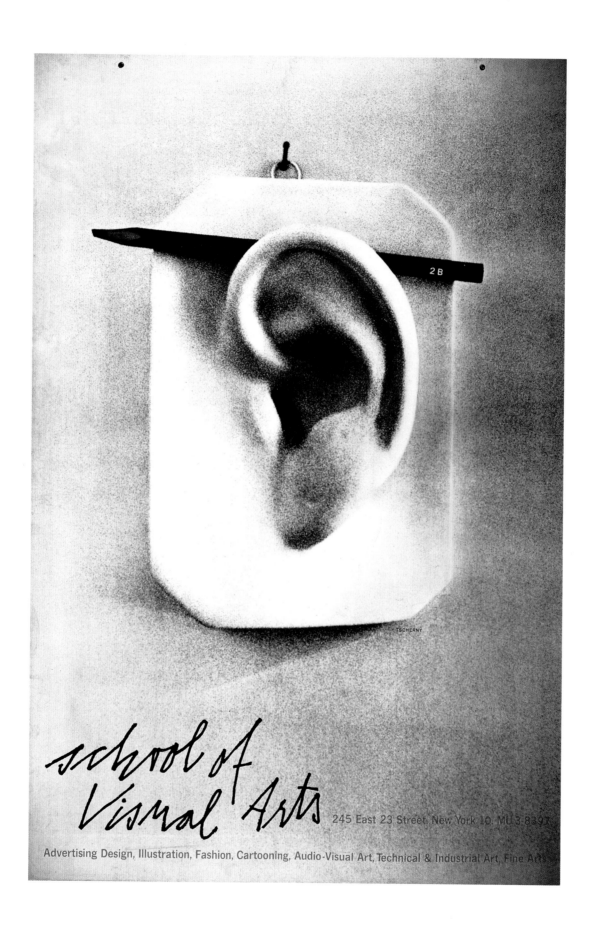

SUBWAY POSTER *Art Director:* Silas H. Rhodes, *Designer:* George Tscherny

"*I remember* so clearly

the effect that *SVA* posters had on me as

a young person, years ago, while traveling

on the subway—never dreaming that one day

my work would be shown there."

DEBORAH SUSSMAN

Partner and Designer, Sussman/Prejza & Co., Inc.

THE sixties

social upheaval and dramatic change affected every aspect of our society in

the sixties. The School of Visual Arts and other educational institutions responsive to the concerns of the times and the needs of

their students reviewed their curriculums and re-examined their approach to teaching. Visual Arts established a Fine Arts

Department and by the end of the decade, galleries exhibiting young artists included a great number of SVA alumni. Team

teaching was initiated, particularly in the applied arts. Considered innovative back then, it was a method that contributed to the

distinct change in the style, shape, look and content of advertising, illustration and design worldwide. This new generation of art

directors, designers, illustrators, photographers and fine artists would shape the vision of communication in the seventies.

The sixties was the youth decade, beginning with the melodic revolutionary music of Bob Dylan and ending with the

celebration of life, love and rock 'n' roll at Woodstock. Young people found a new identity that would shape the course of our

nation's history. Rejecting the fifties' illusion of all's well with the world, our ideas, behavior and values were turned upside

down—too often, violently. Images of John F. Kennedy at the Berlin Wall, "police dogs turned on blacks in Birmingham,

Alabama," burning monks and burning villages in Vietnam were seen in our nation's living rooms with commentary by Walter

Cronkite and David Brinkley. August, 1963 saw 200,000 people come together at the Lincoln Memorial to protest racial injus-

tice and only three months later the assassination of the young President Kennedy threw the nation into a deep sadness and

even deeper cynicism about the capacity of government to make things "all right" ever again. Maturity for the nation would

be severely tested. Lyndon Johnson expanded domestic social programs without reversing Kennedy's major tax cut and

helped launch the spiraling of the national debt.

Martin Luther King's movement for desegregation in the early sixties was a struggling one, but at the March On Washington,

King's "I Have A Dream" speech galvanized ordinary people and racial progress became the cause of the decade continuing

into the next.

The sixties saw the issue of feminism rise out of the low flame of the fifties with Betty Friedan's *The Feminine Mystique*. And

Rachel Carson's *The Silent Spring* confronted the use of pesticides giving environmentalists the hook they needed for a movement.

The Beatles arrived from Liverpool, and the birth control pill, marijuana and acid would be the drugs of choice representing

freedom and a new consciousness and would force a national discussion of personal responsibility and how it translates into

political action. Pop Art—a movement rejecting the conventions of high art and responding to mass culture—brought a new

kind of dealer and collector into art—young, energetic, with money to spend. Television, movies and advertising influenced

Andy Warhol and Roy Lichtenstein—a longtime board member of SVA. They introduced bright, brassy soup and beer cans

and comic imagery to the visual landscape, and art around the world took on a decidedly American look. The movement

revived an interest in comic books, exciting graphic imagery and poster art that would continue right up to today.

The questions of the sixties affected both young and old, uprooted accepted values and challenged all preconceptions. The

questions "blowing in the wind" would have to be answered in the seventies, although many of the answers would remain elusive for

decades to come.

THE SCHOOL OF VISUAL ARTS HAS MOVED TO
ITS NEW ART CENTER / 209-13 E. 23 ST. NYC 10
WRITE OR CALL OFFICE OF ADMISSIONS, MURRAY HILL 3-8397

SUBWAY POSTER *Art Director:* Silas H. Rhodes, *Designer:* Bob Gill, *Photographer:* Ronnie Rojas

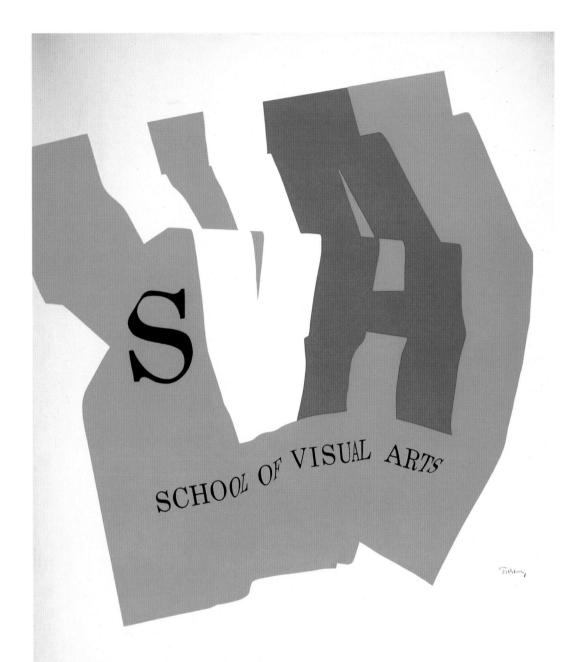

Inside the studios: Renowned professional artists inspire dedicated students. Planned courses encourage creativeness and the search for excellence.   Art becomes a way of life in the professional atmosphere of an independent art school.

Spring Session 1964 – Day & Evening courses: Painting / Drawing / Illustration Sculpture / Printmaking / Photography / Advertising Design / Audio Visual Art Technical Illustration / Journalistic Art / History of Art / Fashion Illustration

Inquire: Office of Admissions   209 East 23 Street, New York 10   MU 3-8397

SUBWAY POSTER *Art Director:* Silas H. Rhodes, *Designer:* George Tscherny, *Copywriter:* Silas H. Rhodes

(REMBRANDT: WAS HE BLIND?)

A TALK BY SALVADOR DALI

AT THE SCHOOL OF VISUAL ARTS 209 EAST 23 ST. THURSDAY FEBRUARY 28th 8:30 PM: ADMISSION FREE: SEATING CAPACITY LIMITED

LECTURE ANNOUNCEMENT *Art Director:* Silas H. Rhodes

Technical
Illustration
Airbrush
Rendering
Photo
Retouching
School of
Visual Arts
209 E. 23 St.
New York 10010
OR 9-7350

SUBWAY POSTER *Art Director:* Silas H. Rhodes, *Designer:* Ivan Chermayeff

Confusion

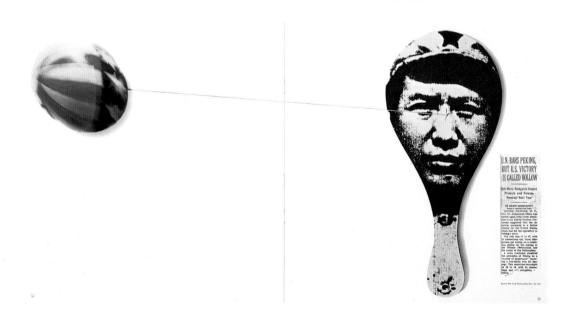

CLASS PROJECT (MAGAZINE) *Art Director:* Henry Wolf

CLASS PROJECT (BOOKLET) *Designer:* Kei Kubo/Assisted by Ina Kershen, *Copywriter:* Silas H. Rhodes, *Instructors:* George Tscherny and Louis Donato

SCHOOL OF VISUAL ARTS
209 EAST 23rd ST./ FOR FURTHER INFORMATION CALL MU 3-8397

SUBWAY POSTER *Art Director:* Silas H. Rhodes, *Illustrator:* Phil Hays

"At SVA

there is a fiery pluralism that I've never found anywhere else. Though I may see things one way and another faculty member may believe the opposite, here we are both tolerated and we are both supported — and so we learn from each other. It's an excellent situation for students and faculty."

LUCIO POZZI

Fine Artist and SVA Instructor

SUBWAY POSTER *Art Director:* Silas H. Rhodes, *Designer:* Tony Palladino

SUBWAY POSTER *Art Director:* Silas H. Rhodes, *Designer:* George Tscherny

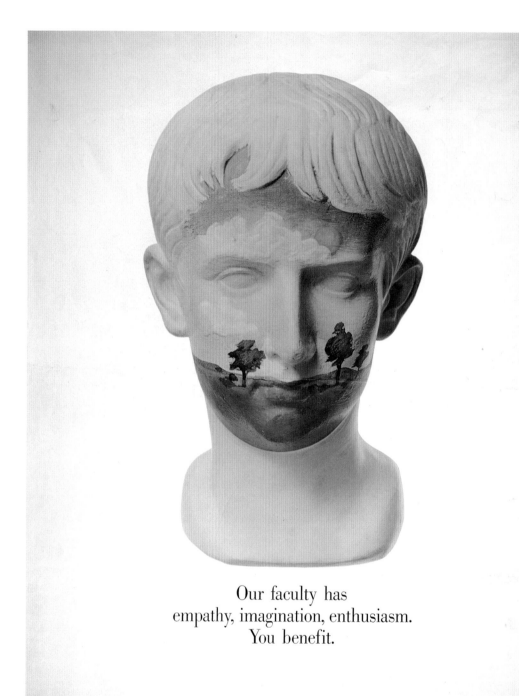

Our faculty has
empathy, imagination, enthusiasm.
You benefit.

Department of Fine Arts: Painting, Drawing, Sculpture, Visual Perception, Printmaking
SCHOOL OF VISUAL ARTS
209 East 23rd Street · New York, New York 10010 · OR 9-7350 · Inquire: Office of Admissions

SUBWAY POSTER *Art Director:* Silas H. Rhodes, *Designer:* Milton Glaser, *Photographer:* Sol Mednick, *Copywriter:* Silas H. Rhodes

MILTON GLASER

" When you design posters for the School of Visual Arts, you are addressing a visual audience, sophisticated and theoretically interested in visual things—an audience, we hope, more capable of dealing with complexity and ambiguity. For them you can do things that stretch human capabilities. All design is contextual and all design begins by considering the audience. If it is not particularly interested in visual things, with no tolerance for ambiguity— you wouldn't use the same forms of address. I believe the work I've done for the School is more adventuresome than anything else I've done, primarily because of the audience. "

Milton Glaser's diverse work produced over the past four decades has at different times not only influenced but is credited with changing the direction of the fields of design and illustration. His close association with Visual Arts has been equally long and his contribution to teaching as influential.

WHAT WERE YOU TRYING TO SAY WITH THIS POSTER IMAGE?

I chose the classical head—purchased at one of those sculpture stores—to represent history. In fact it was very much like one of those heads we used to copy when I was re-learning how to draw while studying in Bologna. I used it to say that the background to creative activity or the arts in general is the history that precedes us. People then come along and impose something different on that background and the meaning changes. Or to say it another way, by rephrasing or imposing something on history, you change its meaning. When you go to school you learn two things: 1) The nature of history and the context out of which you come and (2) how to change that context.

HOW WOULD YOU CHARACTERIZE YOUR LONG RELATIONSHIP WITH THE SCHOOL?

It has been one of the most important parts of my life. I love to teach and I've learned how to do it after twenty years.

My personal friendship with Silas is particularly important to me. He's given me wonderful opportunities to do these posters over the years. I also feel that what the School has done to change the quality of visual life in our times is a profound gift to our culture, perhaps not fully appreciated in a general sense. I've been very happy to be a part of that effort.

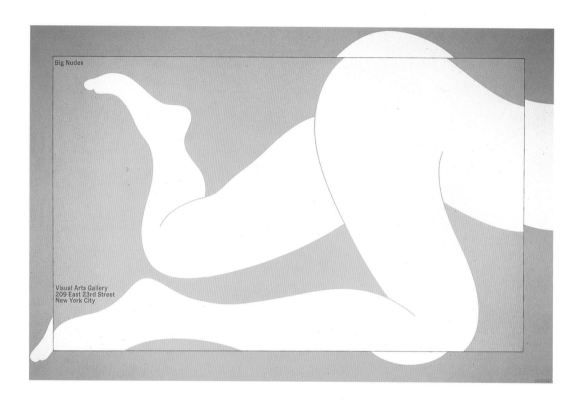

VISUAL ARTS MUSEUM ANNOUNCEMENTS *Art Director:* Silas H. Rhodes, *Designer:* Milton Glaser

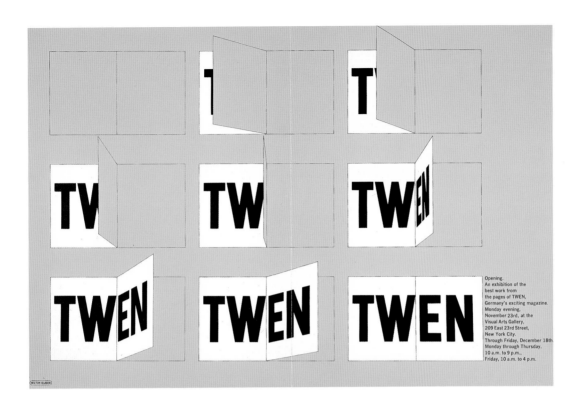

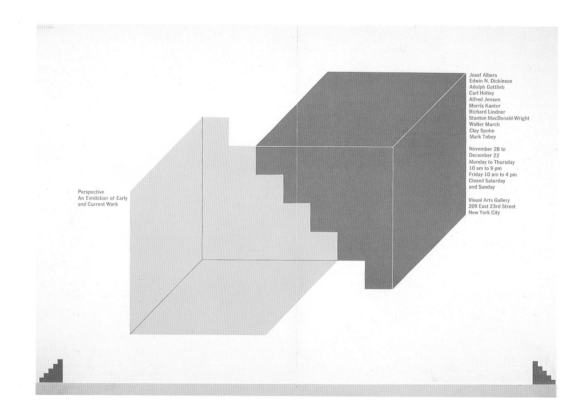

VISUAL ARTS MUSEUM ANNOUNCEMENTS *Art Director:* Silas H. Rhodes, *Designer:* Milton Glaser

An exhibition of 80 extraordinary Polish posters: opening September 16th, 7 p.m. to 10 p.m.

gallery hours 10 a.m. to 9 p.m. Monday, Tuesday, Wednesday, Thursday   10 a.m. to 4 p.m. Friday   Posters collected by Barry Feinstein

The School of Visual Arts 209 East 23rd Street New York City   September 16th through September 30th

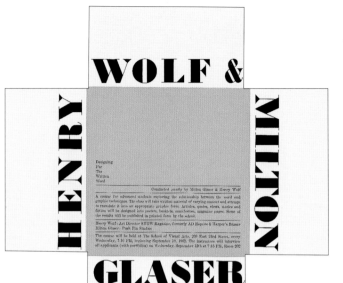

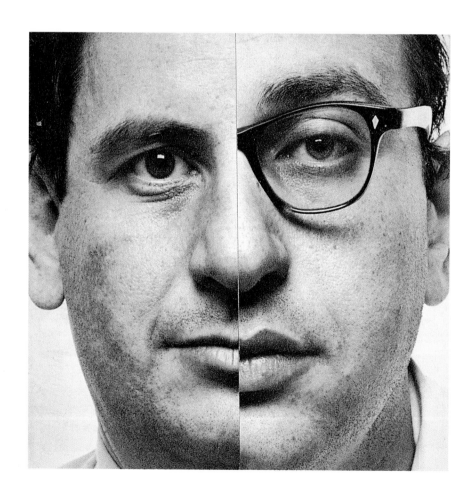

COURSE ANNOUNCEMENT *Art Directors:* Milton Glaser and Henry Wolf

"*The School*

of Visual Arts is a major positive

presence in our field. As a teacher and a

working designer, I have learned a lot

from the young people lucky enough to have

been exposed to its influence."

HENRY WOLF

Hall of Fame Designer and Art Director

CLASS PROJECT ("WONDER" MAGAZINE) *Art Director:* Henry Wolf

6 HEADS ARE BETTER THAN 1
FLIP AND FIND THE WEB-
FOOTED MONKEY DUCK

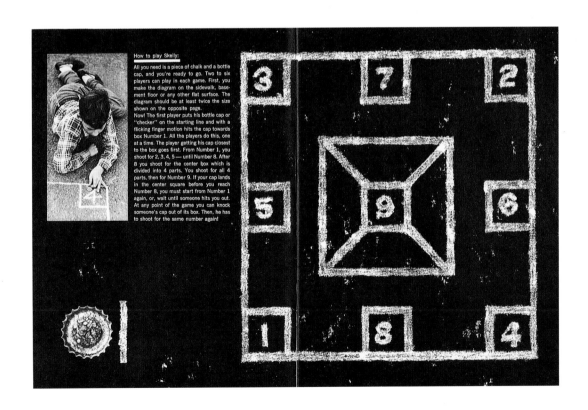

How to play Skelly:

All you need is a piece of chalk and a bottle cap, and you're ready to go. Two to six players can play in each game. First, you make the diagram on the sidewalk, basement floor or any other flat surface. The diagram should be at least twice the size shown on the opposite page.

Now! The first player puts his bottle cap or "checker" on the starting line and with a flicking finger motion hits the cap towards box Number 1. All the players do this, one at a time. The player getting his cap closest to the box goes first. From Number 1, you shoot for 2, 3, 4, 5 — until Number 8. After 8 you shoot for the center box which is divided into 4 parts. You shoot for all 4 parts, then for Number 9. If your cap lands in the center square before you reach Number 8, you must start from Number 1 again, or, wait until someone hits you out. At any point of the game you can knock someone's cap out of its box. Then, he has to shoot for the same number again!

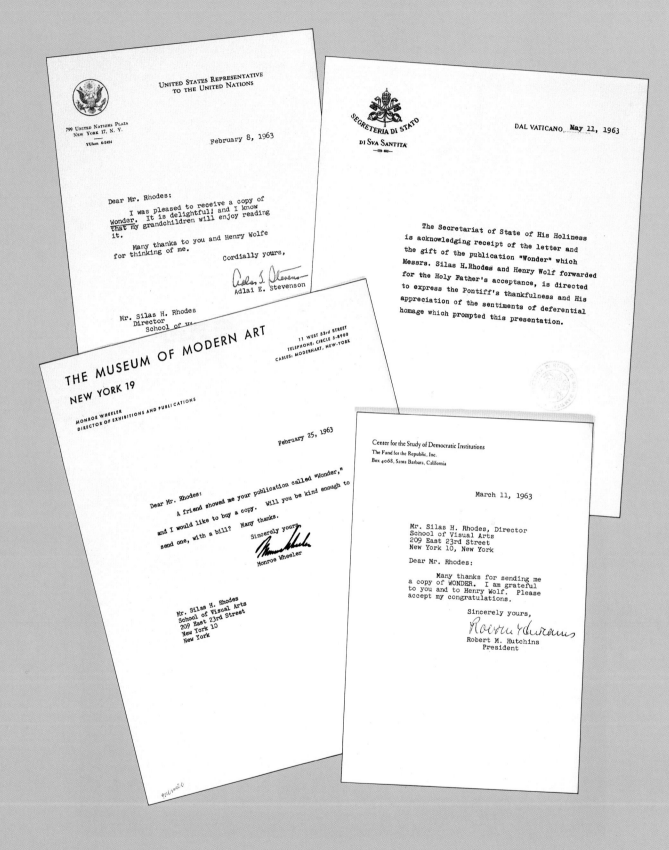

UNITED STATES REPRESENTATIVE
TO THE UNITED NATIONS

799 UNITED NATIONS PLAZA
NEW YORK 17, N. Y.

YUkon 6-2424

February 8, 1963

Dear Mr. Rhodes:

I was pleased to receive a copy of
Wonder. It is delightful! and I know
that my grandchildren will enjoy reading
it.

Many thanks to you and Henry Wolfe
for thinking of me.

Cordially yours,

Adlai E. Stevenson

Mr. Silas H. Rhodes
Director
School of V...

SEGRETERIA DI STATO
DI SVA SANTITA

DAL VATICANO, May 11, 1963

The Secretariat of State of His Holiness
is acknowledging receipt of the letter and
the gift of the publication "Wonder" which
Messrs. Silas H. Rhodes and Henry Wolf forwarded
for the Holy Father's acceptance, is directed
to express the Pontiff's thankfulness and His
appreciation of the sentiments of deferential
homage which prompted this presentation.

THE MUSEUM OF MODERN ART
NEW YORK 19

11 WEST 53RD STREET
TELEPHONE: CIRCLE 5-8900
CABLES: MODERNART, NEW-YORK

MONROE WHEELER
DIRECTOR OF EXHIBITIONS AND PUBLICATIONS

February 25, 1963

Dear Mr. Rhodes:

A friend showed me your publication called "Wonder,"
and I would like to buy a copy. Will you be kind enough to
send one, with a bill? Many thanks.

Sincerely yours,

Monroe Wheeler

Mr. Silas H. Rhodes
School of Visual Arts
209 East 23rd Street
New York 10
New York

Center for the Study of Democratic Institutions
The Fund for the Republic, Inc.
Box 4068, Santa Barbara, California

March 11, 1963

Mr. Silas H. Rhodes, Director
School of Visual Arts
209 East 23rd Street
New York 10, New York

Dear Mr. Rhodes:

Many thanks for sending me
a copy of WONDER. I am grateful
to you and to Henry Wolf. Please
accept my congratulations.

Sincerely yours,

Robert M. Hutchins
President

HARPER'S
BAZAAR

NANCY WHITE, EDITOR

March 1, 1963

Dear Mr. Rhodes:

Please forgive my tardiness in writing to thank
you for my copy of WONDER and to tell you that I think it
is absolutely superb. I returned from Europe to find it
on my desk and was really thrilled...loved every single
moment of it.

My most sincere and heartiest congratulations
to Henry Wolf and to his students. Their "passionate
commitment to excellence" is more than evident. I shall
treasure my copy of WONDER.

Thank you so much.

Most sincerely,

Nancy White

Mr. Silas Rhodes
SCHOOL of VISUAL ARTS

RFF Ruder, Finn & Fujita | Design For Communication
130 East 59th Street, New York 22, N.Y., PL 2-5341

S. Neil Fujita, creative director

February 15, 1963

Mr. Silas H. Rhodes
Director
School of Visual Arts
209 East 23rd Street
New York 10, N. Y.

Dear Silas:

Thank you for the copy of Wonder. It's a fine idea, uniquely
executed, and I enjoyed reading it. Congratulations to you,
Henry, and the staff!

Sincerely,

S. Neil Fujita
S. Neil Fujita

HARVARD UNIVERSITY
CAMBRIDGE 38, MASSACHUSETTS

OFFICE OF THE PRESIDENT

March 13, 1963

Dear Mr. Rhodes:

I was much interested to see the "limited
edition copy" of Wonder. It is a very attractive,
appealing production and must have been an exciting
project. I was particularly interested to see
the article about Le Corbusier, since we are very
proud of our new Carpenter Center building which
was designed by him.

Sincerely yours,

Nathan M. Pusey
Nathan M. Pusey

Mr. Silas H. Rhodes, Director
School of Visual Arts
209 East 23rd Street
New York 10, New York

THE WHITE HOUSE
WASHINGTON

February 19, 1963

Dear Mr. Rhodes:

I have sent up to Mrs. Kennedy the copy of
"Wonder" you and Henry Wolf so graciously sent
her. I know she will be very interested to see it.

Please give my very best to Henry Wolf, and
I congratulate you both on an absolutely fascinating
project.

With all best wishes,

Sincerely,

Letitia Baldrige
Letitia Baldrige
Social Secretary

Mr. Silas H. Rhodes
Director, School of Visual Arts
209 East 23rd Street
New York 10, New York

"Art is a clock that moves too fast when measured by the public's sense of time."
DELACROIX

School of Visual Arts
209 East 23rd Street, New York, New York 10010, OR 9-7350
Courses in commercial art, film art, fine arts.
Inquire: Office of Admissions.

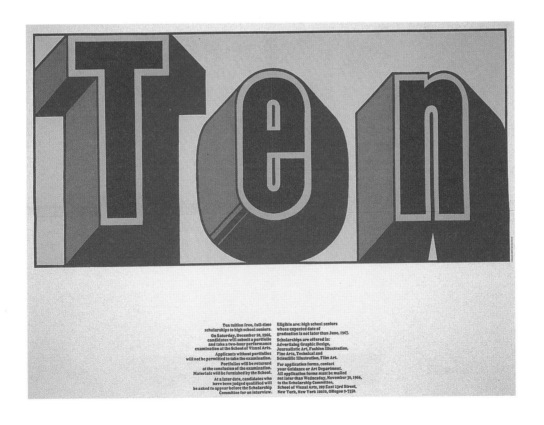

(Top) COURSE ANNOUNCEMENT *Designers:* Tony Palladino and Ivan Chermayeff

(Bottom) SCHOLARSHIP POSTER *Designer:* Cristos Gianakos

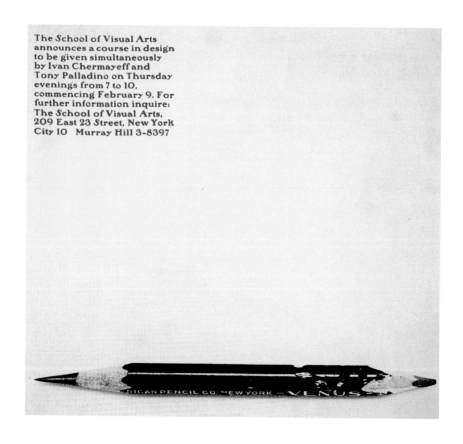

Rendering is not an end in itself, but a vehicle for the communication of ideas. It is upon this principle that Art Harris and Art Kugelman, art directors at Young and Rubicam, and Dave Epstein, free-lance designer, base their course in Layout Techniques. Class begins on Thursday evening, September 26th, 6:40 to 9:40. For information write Office of Admissions, School of Visual Arts, or call MU 3-8397.

The School of Visual Arts
announces a course in design
to be given simultaneously
by Ivan Chermayeff and
Tony Palladino on Thursday
evenings from 7 to 10,
commencing February 9. For
further information inquire:
The School of Visual Arts,
209 East 23 Street, New York
City 10   Murray Hill 3-8397

(Top) COURSE ANNOUNCEMENT *Art Directors:* Art Harris and Art Kugelman, *Designer:* Judith Barrett
(Bottom) COURSE ANNOUNCEMENT *Designers:* Tony Palladino and Ivan Chermayeff

Design by Milton Glaser. Photograph by Alan Vogel

Department of Fine Arts: Painting, Drawing, Sculpture, Visual Perception, Printmaking

SCHOOL OF VISUAL ARTS

209 E. 23rd Street · New York, N.Y. 10010 · OR 9-7350 · Inquire: Office of Admissions

SUBWAY POSTER *Art Director:* Silas H. Rhodes, *Designer:* Milton Glaser, *Photographer:* Alan Vogel

SUBWAY POSTER *Art Director:* Silas H. Rhodes, *Designer:* Milton Glaser, *Photographer:* Peggy Barnett

SUBWAY POSTER *Art Director:* Silas H. Rhodes, *Designer:* Ivan Chermayeff, *Illustrator:* Phil Hays

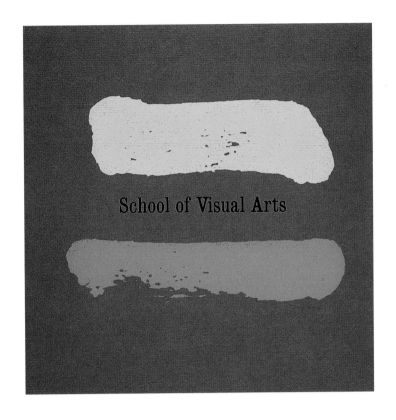

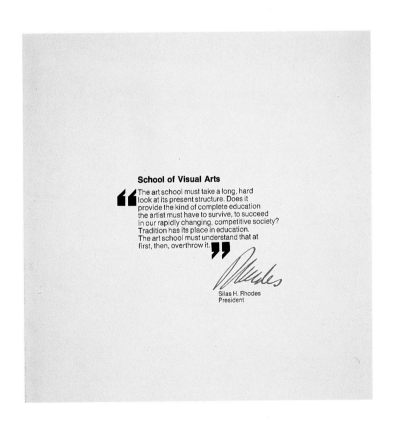

CATALOG COVERS *Art Director:* Silas H. Rhodes, (Top) *Designer:* George Tscherny, (Bottom) *Designer:* Richard Wilde

GEORGE TSCHERNY

" When I did the egg and also the pencil in the ear, it was unusual to see photographic images on posters. Mostly posters were not illustrated but done in a hard edge design—the influence of Cassandra was still in effect. Using photography was really a new way, then. Interestingly enough, I've reversed that a bit—in reaction to the computer. These days I try to avoid technology based solutions when I can. "

George Tscherny's reputation as one of the true innovators of design continues into its fourth decade, but he says "The things that make me happiest are solutions like this poster. I believe it's a perfect example of the visual supporting the verbal—neither one would be as strong without the other." His association with Visual Arts goes back to 1955 when it was known as The Cartoonists and Illustrators School. The first design course he taught began with only 12 students, grew to 50 and then to a whole department.

THIS EMERSON QUOTATION SUGGESTED SOME FAIRLY OBVIOUS SOLUTIONS. WHAT PROMPTED YOU TO MOVE IN THIS DIRECTION?

Well, my initial thinking was kind of naive. I began by literally interpreting the statement and I had images of faces looking between cracks of walls and slightly open doors. But after doing some thinking about it, I realized that the statement was positive and that became the key to the solution. After all, for birds and even for human beings, it all starts behind a wall. It is a very, very positive statement about life.

HOW WAS THE IMAGE PRODUCED?

I'm not a photographer but I can see and that's half of photography—being able to see. So when it comes to doing things like my posters I do my own photography in my studio. I'm not very good about lighting, but for this picture I probably used the natural light coming in from a window. The grainy quality wasn't consciously created, but I photographed it very small on a 35mm slide and then blew it up. It came out very grainy and gave the photo this very interesting characteristic.

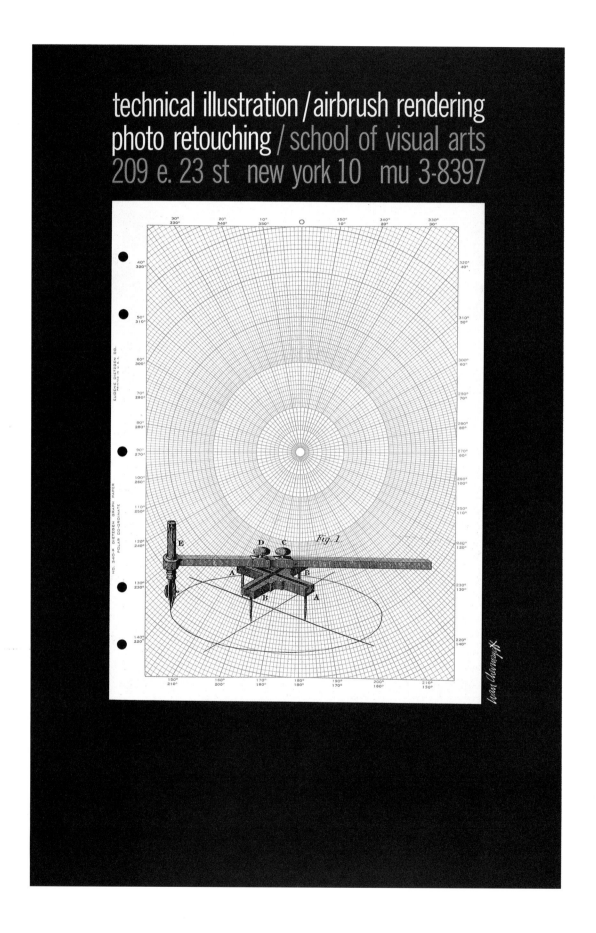

SUBWAY POSTER *Art Director:* Silas H. Rhodes, *Designer:* Ivan Chermayeff

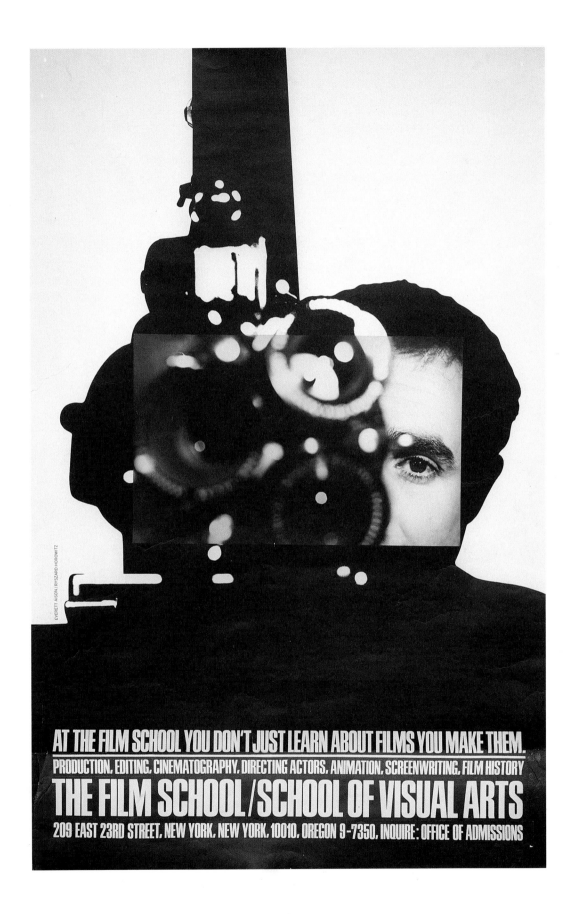

SUBWAY POSTER *Art Director:* Silas H. Rhodes, *Designer:* Everett Aison and Ryszard Horowitz

THE seventies

the direction of the 1970s for the School of Visual Arts was shaped not only by the spirit

of the sixties, but also by a 1972 decision made by The New York State Board of Regents. Visual Arts—after 15 years of negotiations—could finally confer the degree of Bachelor of Fine Arts on graduates of four-year programs in Film, Fine Arts, Media Arts and Photography. And in 1978 the institution also earned accreditation from the Middle States Association of Colleges and Secondary Schools, allowing students to transfer credits to and from all the prominent and established colleges and universities accredited by the Association. The School of Visual Arts could finally begin to activate its educational priorities with the authority it needed to take on a national leadership position on behalf of the arts and all artists. Silas H. Rhodes, the Founder, Director and first President became Chairman, and David Rhodes, Vice President for Academic Affairs, was appointed President. New departments—Art Education and Communication Arts—were established, and opportunities were explored for developing relevant programs abroad in keeping with the growing trend for many American institutions to go international. SVA also opened a professional gallery in Tribeca where student work is exhibited for sale. A Public Advertising System was initiated to create advertising for non-profit organizations as a direct means to contribute to a society that was becoming increasingly pessimistic about its government.

But, if this decade was one of progress for Visual Arts, it was a very difficult one for the nation. High inflation, Watergate, Arab oil embargoes, drugs and violence in the nations' cities and Americans' mistrust of government grew as Richard Nixon became the first president to resign from office. And yet the seventies were also a time when the "transformation of self" was seen as a way to make a difference in society—a concept artists had long ago embraced. The human potential movement caught the attention of the young and middle aged, and encounter groups flourished. More people went back to school to earn professional degrees and women and minorities were able to make strides steadily and quietly.

In the arts, the music was punk. "Saturday Night Live" made its debut. *Jonathan Livingston Seagull* and *The Joy of Sex* topped best-seller lists and minimal and conceptual art changed art consciousness, once again. Minimalists stripped art back to essentials and conceptual art sought to eliminate objects completely. Joseph Kossuth and Mel Bochner—both on the Visual Arts faculty—along with Lawrence Wiener and Dan Graham were in the forefront of the movement. Earth Artists, too, were determined to wipe out easel painting. But meanwhile, figurative and representational artists simply retreated to their studios, away from the fray, to work in peace until their time came around again. The commercial arts—advertising, graphic design and illustration—as always, responded directly to the changes in music and the fine arts by producing sophisticated work and striking imagery.

By decade's end it was clear that we would have to learn to live with struggle and turmoil as a norm and people were determined to remain optimistic, to do what they could to take care of "me." Consequently, self-improvement, education, meditation and running were ways of achieving inner peace in lieu of being able to make any impact on the events of the world outside.

SUBWAY POSTER *Art Director:* Gene Case, *Copywriter:* Gene Case

"*After* getting out of the Navy,

I started wrapping packages in Benton &

Bowles with a desire to get into advertising.

I was advised by a few art directors to take a

night course from the professionals at the SVA

night school. Lessons I have never forgotten,

and are the cornerstone for much of the success

I have attained today."

MARTIN PEDERSON

Designer and CEO *Graphis*

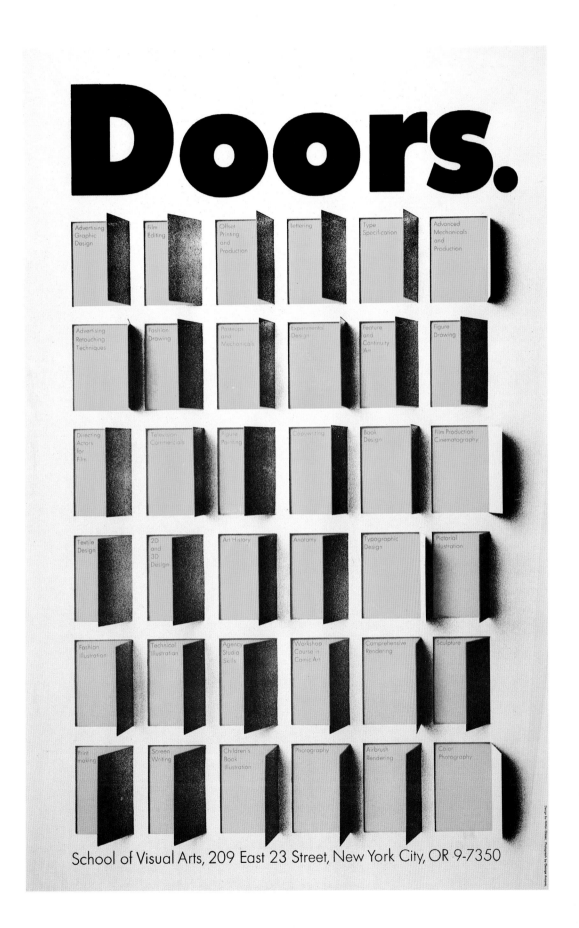

SUBWAY POSTER *Art Director:* Silas H. Rhodes, *Designer:* Milton Glaser, *Photographer:* George Ancona, *Copywriter:* Silas H. Rhodes

To be good is not enough, when you dream of being great.

Degree and Non-Degree Programs. Day and Evening. Film, Photography, Media Arts (Advertising, Copy Writing, Fashion, Illustration, Graphic Design), Crafts (Ceramics, Jewelry), Fine Arts (Painting, Sculpture, Printmaking), Video Tape, Dance, Humanities, Art Education, Art Therapy.

School of Visual Arts
School of Visual Arts, 209 East 23rd Street, New York City 10010 (212) 683-0600

SUBWAY POSTER *Art Director:* Silas H. Rhodes, *Illustrator:* Robert Weaver, *Copywriter:* Dee Ito

School of Visual Arts

SUBWAY POSTER *Art Director:* Silas H. Rhodes, *Designer:* Richard Wilde, *Illustrator:* Robert Giusti

When you've seen one,
you've seen one.

SCHOOL OF VISUAL ARTS
209 East 23rd Street, New York, N.Y. OR 9-7350
250 courses in Photography, Film, Technical & Fantastic Illustration, Fashion, Advertising, Illustration, Fine Arts.

SUBWAY POSTER *Art Director:* Silas H. Rhodes, *Designer:* Sal DeVito, *Photographer:* Charles Wiesehahn, *Copywriter:* Sal DeVito

S A L   D E V I T O

❝ I was 21 years old and had just graduated from Visual Arts. It was my first day going to my first job at an agency called Conahay and Lyon. I bought my subway token and went through the gate. And then, there it was! My poster right there on the platform! I said 'Wow!' I mean I really flipped—it was the very first thing I'd ever produced and I had never seen it before. But to see it like that—on my way to work—it was really cool. You always remember your first. ❞

Sal DeVito has the distinction of being the only Visual Arts student to do a poster for the School while he was a student. Now as Creative Director of his own agency with partner Ellis Verdi—he produces award-winning campaigns for clients like Daffy's—a discount clothing store—and Solgar Vitamins. Recently, DeVito/Verdi received the 4A's award for Best Small Agency of the Year. DeVito has been teaching at SVA since 1980 and very often hires his own students after graduation to work for him at the agency.

WHAT WAS THE STORY BEHIND THE PRODUCTION OF THIS POSTER?

I was still in school then. And at that time, every year the senior class in Advertising was assigned the problem of doing an ad for The School of Visual Arts to appear in *Art Direction Magazine*. And as seniors, it was finally our turn. Chet Lane and Ed Bianchi—who were both teaching at SVA at the time—gave us the assignment. Each of us worked on our ads individually—it wasn't a team project. When Chet and Ed saw my ad I guess they thought it was a nice concept, but they never said, "this is the one" or anything like that. But, a few days later, Bob Giraldi—he was head of the Advertising Department—contacted me and said, "I heard about the ad you did. Let's do it." That was such a terrific moment for me. Bob had a great deal to do with getting it produced. He took me through the whole process. He invited me to come over to DellaFemina—where he was at that time—and he asked Charlie Wiesehahn to shoot the photograph for us. Then, Bob supervised me doing the mechanical—I didn't know enough about type and things like that to do it on my own. But when it was finished, Silas saw it and I heard he really liked it a lot and he said, "blow it up for a subway poster" and that was it. That's how my ad became a poster. It was a major event in my life.

PASSION (MAGAZINE), CLASS PROJECT *Art Directors/Instructors:* Milton Glaser and Henry Wolf

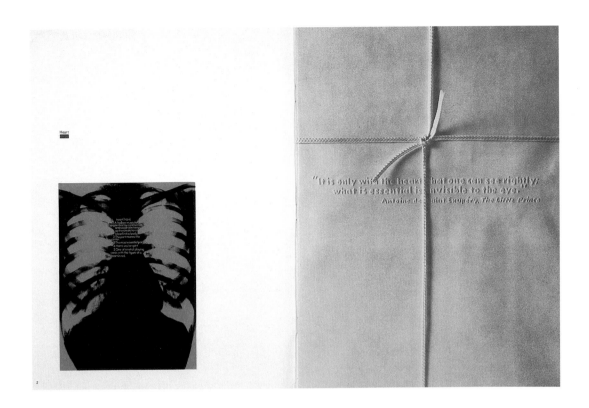

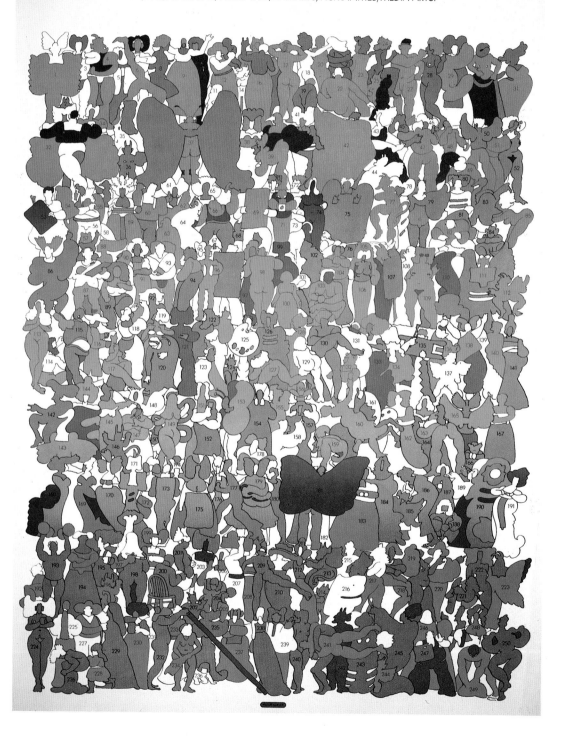

PAUL DAVIS

" The thing that gave me the most pride when I was a student at The School of Visual Arts was seeing George Tscherny's posters in the subway. I mean no other school had that presence. And even today there is still no other art school that has the graphic presence of Visual Arts. When you see the work that represents the institution, you know it practices what it preaches. If you're an art school that teaches design and advertising, you have no right to put up materials that are not the very best. But there are lots of schools that don't even come close. What it means to me is that they don't know any better—they don't get it. But if they don't get it, the question is, how can they teach it? The more I know about schools and education the more of an enthusiast I am about Visual Arts. "

Paul Davis's impressive achievements in the fields of design and illustration earned him the election to The New York Art Director's Club Hall of Fame in 1995—its highest honor. Davis shows his paintings in three international galleries— *Il Gabbiano* and *Nuages* in Italy and *The Nishimura Gallery* in Japan. He is on the graduate faculty of SVA's *Illustration As Visual Essay* Master's program, *The Drawing Room*, a publication focused on drawing which was initiated by illustrator, Robert Weaver.

WHAT INSPIRED YOUR SOLUTION FOR THIS POSTER?

It was a very tough headline to deal with. It's very specific and I find it's always easier to deal with lines that are more ambiguous, but I started looking through some reference pictures while thinking about aspirations, hopes and dreams. And I came across a photograph of Yvette Gilbert taken about 1925—some 30 years after she was painted by Toulouse Lautrec. The Lautrec picture was of a smiling, skinny woman holding back a curtain with a worldly, cynical look on her face. You knew she had seen it all, been through it all. But this photograph showed a chubby woman who had an innocent look, a kind of almost naive sweet hope on her face. I loved the idea of painting Lautrec's subject, but from a totally different perspective. I was trying for a classical poster and a classical image. She had that kind of yearning I was after. The background with the stars and the moon is one I've used before to visualize the kinds of hopes that aim at the stars, that go beyond, out into space. And those were all the elements I needed to make the image.

SUBWAY POSTER *Art Director:* Silas H. Rhodes, *Designer/Illustrator:* Paul Davis, *Copywriter:* Dee Ito

SUBWAY POSTER *Art Director:* Silas H. Rhodes, *Designer:* Milton Glaser, *Copywriter:* Dee Ito

TALENT IS HER BUSINESS

Eileen McClash runs one of the most unique operations in the college placement field, The School of Visual Arts Talent Agency. The agency represents the talented students and graduates of S.V.A. And there's never a fee. Eileen is widely experienced in all areas of the Visual Arts. She makes every effort to put the right artist with the right job. She assists students in finding part-time employment if they need it. And of course, keeps constant contact with prospective employers so S.V.A. graduates have first crack at good jobs when they become available. Eileen finds that her placement efforts are made easier because of the school's reputation for producing great work. Our students exhibit in major competitions across the country, and often walk away with prizes. Having a talent isn't worth much, unless you know what to do with it. Eileen's students have put their talents in her hands, she puts their talents in your jobs.

The School of Visual Arts Talent Agency, Inc.
209 East 23rd Street, New York, New York 10010/212-679-7350

Design: Richard Wilde, Photo: Stan Shaffer

SVA PLACEMENT AGENCY ADVERTISEMENT: *Art Director:* Silas H. Rhodes, *Designer:* Richard Wilde, *Photographer:* Stan Shaffer

JAMES McMULLAN

" Doing a poster for the School is much more liberating and more demanding than executing the usual assignment because with Silas you have a very sophisticated client. You know it's going to take something ingenious to catch his fancy. And that's terrific. I mean what more would you want than to really outdo yourself and make the effort to come up with something really interesting and personal. "

Jim McMullan's work in illustration is highly regarded for its innovative approach to drawing. He has taught illustration at Visual Arts for the past 25 years and in 1994 his definitive process book, *High Focus Drawing*, was published based on his experiences in the classroom. He and his wife, Kate, also collaborate on doing one children's book each year. He is particularly proud of their most recent book, *Hey, Pipsqueak*.

THE APPLE IMAGE WAS VERY STRIKING. DID IT COME TO YOU IMMEDIATELY?

Actually, no. I often have to work through some very obvious ideas in order to get rid of them. But once I realized that the line referred to the big idea of doing something that would make your career—go for the gold and all that—I decided that Manhattan was not only where you were trained for success, but where you'd probably find it. You know, it was a jazz term out of the twenties. When musicians talked about playing the Big Apple, they meant Manhattan. I'm fairly certain that it was this SVA poster that brought it back as an image for the city. I was also working with a lot of ideas about maps and diagrams then and the poster flowed out of them. Then, too, I was interested in flatness and illusion—I still am. The water sort of curls up at you at the bottom. The map glamourizes New York as the center of all activity and the lucky neighbors get a little bit of red glow from the apple.

DID YOU GET ANY OTHER RESPONSES TO THE POSTER?

Well, some people really took offense because somehow I managed to leave out Brooklyn. I thought vaguely that there was sort of a hierarchy and that Brooklyn was in the hierarchy of Queens. Anyway, I received quite a few calls and I had no answer. I was guilty. It went through the whole process and no one noticed. In some of the subway stations, people wrote Brooklyn in—it became the graffiti.

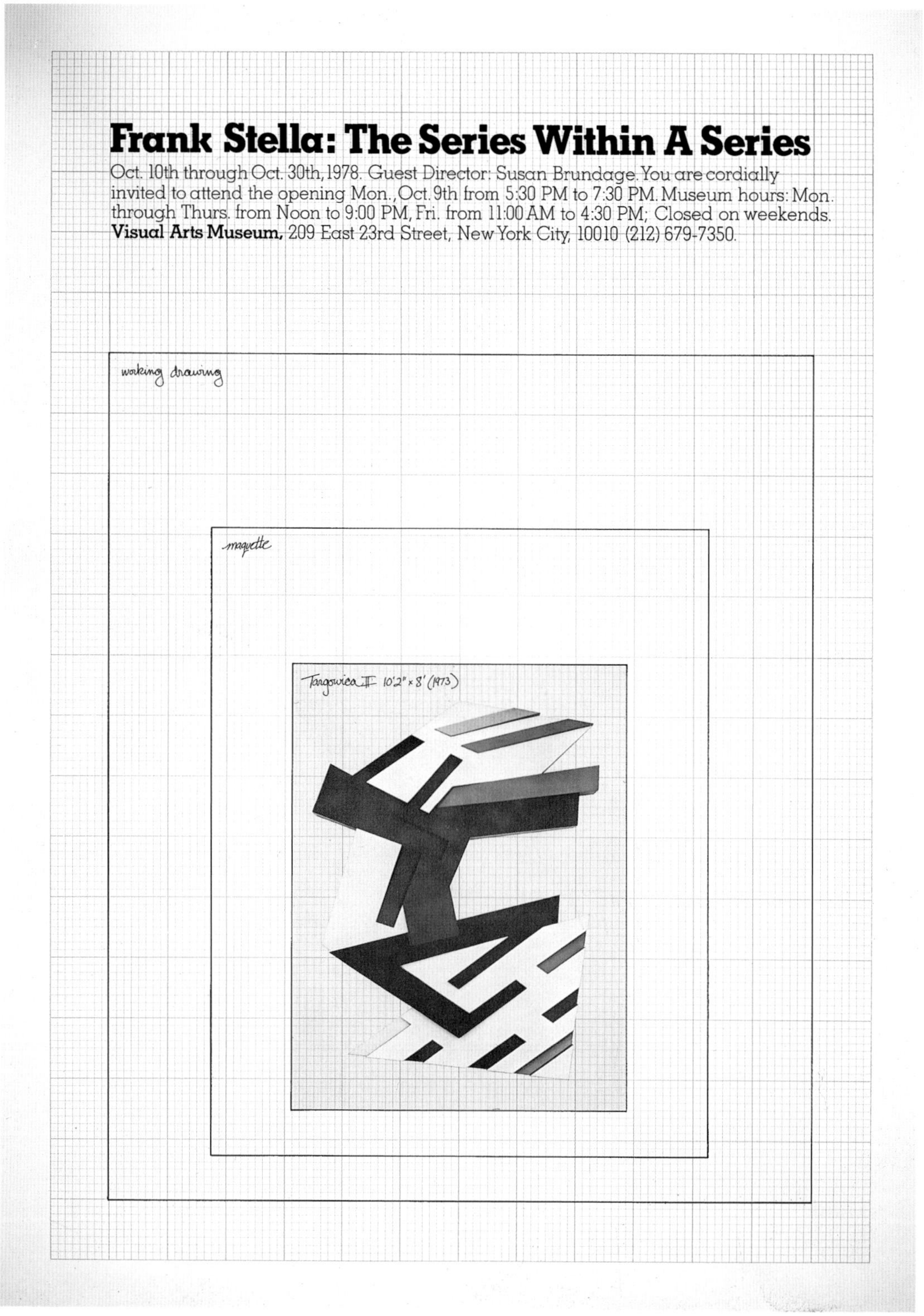

Frank Stella: The Series Within A Series

Oct. 10th through Oct. 30th, 1978. Guest Director: Susan Brundage. You are cordially
invited to attend the opening Mon., Oct. 9th from 5:30 PM to 7:30 PM. Museum hours: Mon.
through Thurs. from Noon to 9:00 PM, Fri. from 11:00 AM to 4:30 PM; Closed on weekends.
Visual Arts Museum, 209 East 23rd Street, New York City, 10010 (212) 679-7350.

working drawing

maquette

Targowica II 10'2" × 8' (1973)

VISUAL ARTS MUSEUM ANNOUNCEMENT *Creative Director:* Silas H. Rhodes, *Art Director:* Richard Wilde, *Designer:* Diane Addesso

VISUAL ARTS MUSEUM ANNOUNCEMENT *Art Director:* Silas H. Rhodes, *Designer/Illustrator:* Paul Davis

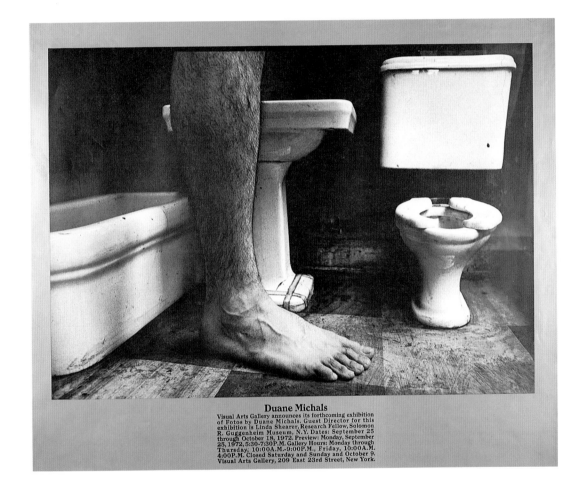

Duane Michals
Visual Arts Gallery announces its forthcoming exhibition of Fotos by Duane Michals. Guest Director for this exhibition is Linda Shearer, Research Fellow, Solomon R. Guggenheim Museum, N.Y. Dates: September 25 through October 18, 1972. Preview: Monday, September 25, 1972, 5:30-7:30P.M. Gallery Hours: Monday through Thursday, 10:00A.M.-9:00P.M., Friday, 10:00A.M. 4:00P.M. Closed Saturday and Sunday and October 9. Visual Arts Gallery, 209 East 23rd Street, New York.

VISUAL ARTS MUSEUM ANNOUNCEMENT *Art Director:* Silas H. Rhodes, *Designer:* Richard Wilde, *Photographer:* Duane Michals

"*Do the* SVA students *know how lucky they are to be in the design and art capital of the world and to be taught by the best practitioners who are available, because they work in the design and art capital of the world?*"

SEYMOUR CHWAST

Designer and Co-Founder, PUSHPIN GROUP

VISUAL ARTS MUSEUM ANNOUNCEMENT *Art Director:* Silas H. Rhodes, *Photographer:* Hans Namuth

Robert Weaver: Retrospective 1956-1977

Opening January 5th, 1977 5-8 PM. January 5th, 1977 through January 21th, 1977. Guest Director:
Marshall Arisman. Museum Hours: Monday — Thursday 12 PM — 9 PM • Friday 11 AM — 4:30 PM.
Closed Weekends. Visual Arts Museum • 209 East 23rd Street New York City 10010 • 212-679-7350

VISUAL ARTS MUSEUM ANNOUNCEMENT *Creative Director:* Silas H. Rhodes, *Designer:* Richard Wilde, *Illustrator:* Robert Weaver

Spend a few nights with us. It may change the way you spend the rest of your days.

Degree and Non-Degree Programs
Film, Photography, Media Arts (Advertising, Fashion, Illustration, Design)
Fine Arts (Painting, Sculpture, Printmaking, Crafts), Video Tape

School of Visual Arts
209 East 23rd Street, New York, N.Y. 10010 · 679-7350

SUBWAY POSTER *Art Director:* Silas H. Rhodes, *Designer:* Richard Wilde, *Artist:* Audrey Flack, *Copywriter:* Dick Wasserman

TONY PALLADINO

"The pros think that the solution to design is technology, that the message lies in the excitement of what you put down on the surface, rather than the idea—that's at the root of redundancy we see around us. There are hardly any ideas out there. That's rather sad. People are not attuned to getting graphic ideas, except maybe when they go to the movies. Even then, the bombardment of images is oriented toward what's going to sell."

Tony Palladino is a concept-oriented art director who can draw—his fine artwork has been exhibited in many galleries. Also, as a communications and advertising consultant he is called on by agencies and clients such as Mobil Oil and Masterpiece Theater for strategy and problem solving. He teaches a course in Communication Design and has been on the SVA faculty for over 25 years.

THIS WAS SUCH A SIMPLE, ACCURATE SOLUTION TO A POTENTIALLY DIFFICULT ILLUSTRATION PROBLEM. WHAT WAS THE SOURCE FOR THE INSPIRATION?

It was such a beautiful line. I thought I really have to do something special with it. The concept came right from the street, from Harlem and that is, if you don't take care of what you've got that's positive—and in this case it's talent—you'll just screw yourself and end up with zip, with nothing. The image of the pencil pushing into the eraser and forming a zero said it perfectly and I didn't try for anything else. When I was doing the drawing for the sketch, I thought it was wonderful, so I knew I had to do a drawing for the finish. I also thought it might be nice to show students that drawing actually takes place in this school. I always let the concept tell me what to do. I choose the medium—drawing or painting—depending on the idea.

WHAT THOUGHTS DO YOU HAVE ABOUT DOING POSTERS, IN GENERAL?

A poster has to work on a 3- or 4-second take. I always try to come up with a single image that works with the headline. If an illustration or design becomes too involved, then forget about it—the poor line has no life. Posters demand simplicity. They are about hit and run.

SCHOOL OF VISUAL ARTS 209 EAST 23rd STREET, NEW YORK, NEW YORK 10010
DAY SCHOOL (212)679-7350. DIVISION OF CONTINUING EDUCATION (212)683-0600
DEGREE AND NON-DEGREE PROGRAMS, DAY, EVENING AND SATURDAY SESSIONS. FILM, ART EDUCATION, PHOTOGRAPHY, MEDIA ARTS (ADVERTISING, FASHION, ILLUSTRATION, DESIGN, ART THERAPY), CRAFTS (CERAMICS, JEWELRY), FINE ARTS (PAINTING, SCULPTURE, PRINTMAKING), VIDEO TAPE, HUMANITIES.

Having a talent isn't worth much unless you know what to do with it.

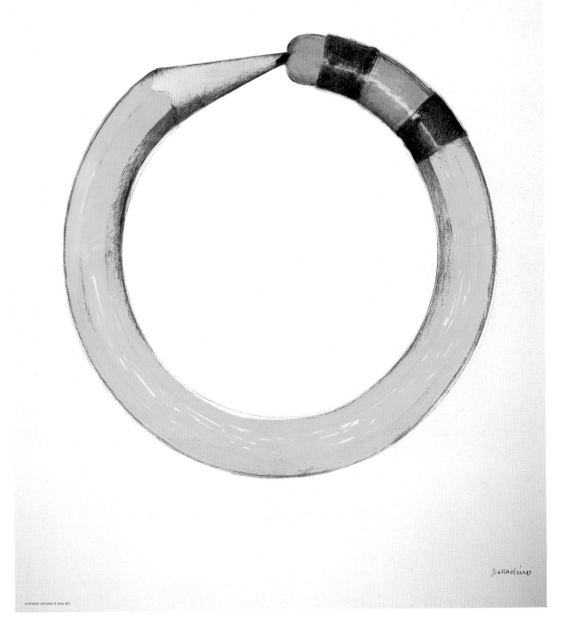

SUBWAY POSTER *Art Director:* Silas H. Rhodes, *Designer/Illustrator:* Tony Palladino, *Copywriter:* Dee Ito

THE eighties

the history

books will designate the 1980's in this country as the era of the computer revolution—40 million of them sold to Americans. And the School of Visual Arts was in the first wave. Recognizing the computer's vast potential as an artistic tool, SVA established one of the very first computer graphics centers in the world. Students use and experiment with the most technologically advanced computer graphics hardware and software in an art context.

The eighties also saw the approval by the New York State Board of Regents for a graduate degree program for Master of Fine Arts in Computer Art, the first program of its kind in the United States. Master of Fine Arts degrees in Illustration and Fine Arts were also approved during these years. The eighties—working off the input of the School's research in the seventies—marked the launch of Visual Arts' first Summer International Program in Morocco, Ireland and Italy, and the success of this ambitious undertaking was mirrored in the America of the eighties.

Technological advances and unprecedented economic expansion marked the decade. There were 118 million jobs by 1990. More women were working and the two-paycheck family became the norm with women's earning power growing each year. Even though parity was not achieved, feminists continued to push for equal pay for equal work and a constitutional equal rights amendment. AIDS, homelessness and the rise of the religious right would also contribute to the change in the social and political reality of the upcoming decade.

Business was transformed with high-yield bonds named by Michael Milken as "junk bonds"—safely used in the seventies to underwrite fast growing companies—but used in the eighties to take over vulnerable corporations that would yield vast turnaround profits. The arts community saw the decade begin with a tragedy—John Lennon's death. But the eighties also saw musicians use their popularity and influence to organize Live AID—an international benefit to support famine relief in Africa. They raised $70 million worldwide. Cable television became a force changing the face of mass culture and Madonna became a star. The content of popular culture shifted to accommodate more sex and violence.

Fine Art underwent even more change in the high-flying eighties and prices for modern painting and sculpture soared, although by the end of the eighties the market for art as well as stocks had dropped out. Public art made its debut in the eighties. Maya Lin's Vietnam Veteran's Memorial, Christo's *Surrounded Islands* and Richard Serra's *Tilted Arc* caused anger and controversy, and the Postmodern movement challenged some of the fundamental ideas of modern art and architecture. Art terms like deconstruction, appropriation and simulation were introduced into our vocabularies, but it was the ideas they represented that would affect the vision, the trends and even the way society thinks. Postmodernists claim that authorship is dead, that thoughts and images are collective and that no one owns them. On the publishing front, the look and feel of books, magazines and printed matter changed dramatically. Computer type and computer imagery exploded and more designers and illustrators recognized that not only was change within their fields inevitable, it may already have happened.

SUBWAY POSTER *Art Director:* Silas H. Rhodes, *Designer:* William J. Kobasz, *Illustrator:* Robert Weaver, *Copywriter:* Dee Ito

SUBWAY POSTER *Art Director:* Silas H. Rhodes, *Designer:* Paula Scher

"*The* School of Visual Arts affords the greatest possibility for a well-informed design education, as it is staffed with the best working professionals in graphic design as faculty.

The informed student can be guided through the graphic design department to find the most suitable education. The possibilities are limitless."

PAULA SCHER, PARTNER

Pentagram Design, Inc.

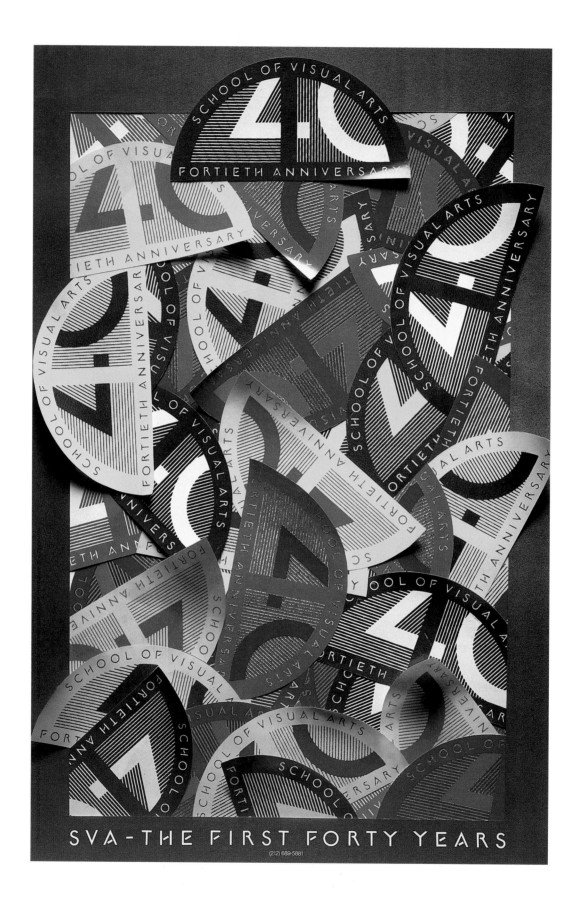

SUBWAY POSTER *Art Director:* Silas H. Rhodes, *Designer:* Milton Glaser

SUBWAY POSTER *Art Director:* Silas H. Rhodes, *Painting:* Marshall Arisman

SUBWAY POSTER *Art Director:* Silas H. Rhodes, *Painting:* Paul Waldman

SUBWAY POSTER *Art Director:* Silas H. Rhodes, *Designer:* William J. Kobasz, *Illustrator:* Marvin Mattelson, *Copywriter:* Dee Ito

MARVIN MATTELSON

" Doing a poster for Visual Arts was a very significant thing for me. The artists who had previously created posters set a very high standard. I felt really pressured to come up with something that reflected the true meaning of the headline. You know, if I had to choose a credo for myself as a person and as an artist—the headline was written for me. I'm never satisfied with anything. I take everything to the next level possible. I always want it to be better and greater. The classic zebra was a definition of myself. "

Marvin Mattelson's illustrations are widely seen in every major magazine, but the range of his work extends to books, portraits and "weird surrealist paintings." His distinctive cover image for the compact disc of *Chant*—the hugely successful album of Gregorian chants—is significantly credited for selling 7 million copies worldwide. It earned him a platinum record.

THE RAINBOW ZEBRA IS SUCH A DISTINCTIVE IMAGE. HOW LONG DID IT TAKE FOR YOU TO DECIDE IT WAS THE RIGHT ONE?

I started with a specific direction suggested by Silas—circus imagery—and I tried to come up with something along the lines of that theme. I had a very long deadline—six months—so Murphy's Law took over and I took the amount of time I was given to find the solution. Even when I came up with the zebra and knew it was right, it was just the beginning. I then literally went for months doing sketches of rainbow zebras in galleries, rainbow zebras on canvasses hanging in galleries, rainbow zebras in subways. I mean, rainbow zebras in every configuration, possible.

HOW DID YOU DECIDE ON THE BLACK AND WHITE SHADOW?

The shadow was the quintessential part of the painting. The rainbow zebra, I felt, symbolized greatness, meaning going beyond what is expected. I started out trying to paint a very complicated picture that would show up my technical skills. I mean, I was looking for a way to do a great painting in addition to a great image. But as I did the final sketch, I knew it was right to do the zebra against no-seam casting a shadow to create dimension. But as I started putting it in, it hit me that the shadow should be the black and white zebra.

Being "good" was very flat, compared to "great" which is multidimensional. It was exactly what I was looking for when I was trying all those backgrounds that didn't work.

SUBWAY POSTER *Art Director:* Silas H. Rhodes, *Designer:* William J. Kobasz, *Illustrator:* Barbara Nessim

SVA FILM SCHOOL EXHIBITION POSTERS *Designers:* Elizabeth Barret and Sheri Lee, *Illustrator:* Jose Ortega

"*Aside* from the technical knowledge, the unique benefit of an SVA education is that teachers at SVA are working professionals who teach about how the art business works. Only a working pro can lead you into the profession."

JOE QUESADA
Comic Artist, Publisher, SVA Graduate

SUBWAY POSTER *Art Director:* Silas H. Rhodes, *Designer/Copywriter:* Tony Palladino

SCHOOL OF VISUAL ARTS

SUBWAY POSTER *Art Director:* Silas H. Rhodes, *Designer:* Richard Wilde, *Artist:* Don Eddy

EXHIBITION POSTER *Creative Director:* Silas H. Rhodes, *Art Directors:* Richard Wilde/David Connolly, *Designer:* Amy Cordell, *Copywriter:* Judith Wilde, *Illustrator:* Frank Frisari

The School of Visual Arts presents Halley's Comet: Past, Present and Future, an exhibition of a sampling of comet sightings by its students, at The Master Eagle Gallery, 40 West 25th Street, sixth floor, Thursday, March 13 through Wednesday, May 7, 1986, Monday through Friday, 9:30a.m. to 4:30p.m. ....·

HALLEY'S COMET

School of Visual Arts
In cooperation with The Master Eagle Family of Companies

EXHIBITION POSTER *Creative Director:* Silas H. Rhodes, *Art Directors:* Richard Wilde/William J. Kobasz, *Designers:* William J. Kobasz/Robin Gillmore-Barnes, *Illustrator:* Jose Ortega

J E R R Y   M O R I A R T Y

" *I had a choice of two poster lines and I liked 'To Be Good Is Not Enough, When You Dream of Being Great' and I intended to visualize it literally. But when I was talking with Bob Weaver—who had done many posters—he said, 'You don't have to do that. The line is just put on the poster.' But it's what I wanted to do—illustrate the words, so I ignored his advice. It's the illustrator's challenge to say what the words mean to me.* "

P ainter, illustrator, writer, cartoonist Jerry Moriarty wrote and illustrated the classic *Jack Survives*, A Raw Publication. He has also written and illustrated 100 stories called *Visual Crimes*. Currently, he is working on a series of paintings about buffalo and his cat for his anticipated Moriarty Memorial Exhibit some 20 or 40 years from now.

HOW DID YOU ARRIVE AT THE ILLUSTRATION THAT BECAME THIS POSTER?

The first consideration was that it had to be vertical. So, I thought about three levels—the person at street level would look straight into the middle of the poster, then look up and look down. *Jack Survives* was done in three tiers so I had a reference point even though I'd stopped doing the strip a couple of years before. At the time, I was illustrating men's adventure stories, writing them, too. And that's where the concept of the color came from. I was using one color and grey—a style used in the fifties of printing color cheaply. I was originally going to do the poster in one color. I was thinking of orange because of evening school—the sun setting and all. But Silas said, "we've had trouble with orange because the fluorescent light cancels the color out, so why don't you run down to the subway and see if it reads." I ended up doing it in orange, but it looked pale so I went to blue as a complement and I kept the grey. All the darks and lights of the orange are grey and they change to brown when you put grey in it, and the blues also change when you add grey.

Interpreting the headline, I had the challenge of the sign painter looking into the window of the fine artist and Jack down below who is only interested in the coffee cup painting of the sign painter—he's everyman, nowhere near art. The sign painter is like the illustrator and the fine artist is inside. The poster was the hardest thing I'd done up to that time because it was going to Silas. I was in absolute awe of him. I wanted him to be happy. He looked at it and said, "that's great," which was the word I was illustrating. It was the casual way he said it that cracked me up.

SUBWAY POSTER *Creative Director:* Silas H. Rhodes, *Designer:* William J. Kobasz, *Illustrator:* Jerry Moriarty, *Copywriter:* Dee Ito

STATIONERY SYSTEM *Creative Director:* Silas H. Rhodes, *Designer:* William J. Kobasz

40TH ANNIVERSARY LOGO *Designer:* Milton Glaser

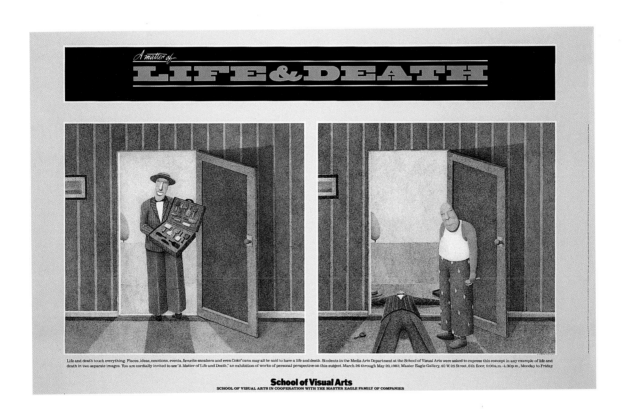

EXHIBITION POSTER   *Art Director:* Richard Wilde, *Designers:* William J. Kobasz/Susan Spivak, *Illustrator:* Paul Yalowitz

SUBWAY POSTER *Creative Director:* Silas H. Rhodes, *Designer:* William J. Kobasz, *Illustrator:* James McMullan, *Copywriter:* Dee Ito

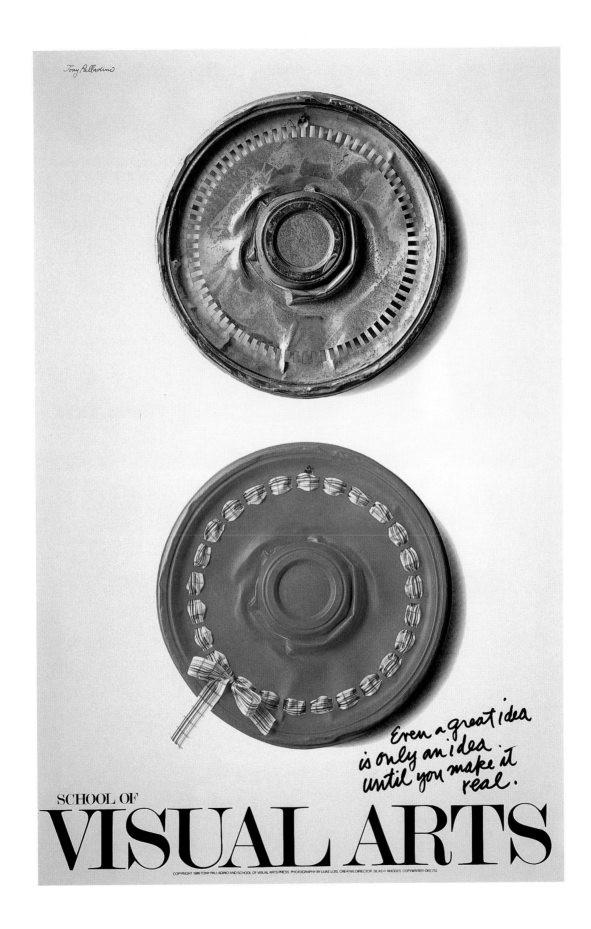

MOROCCO

SCHOOL OF VISUAL ARTS
SUMMER IN MOROCCO

An extraordinary summer in Tangier studying Drawing, Painting, Photography, Creative Writing or Islamic Culture and Art. Spend three weeks or six weeks.

First Session: July 3–July 24
Second Session: July 24–August 14
Faculty:
Photography—David Attie, Abby Robinson
Painting—Bruce Boice, Michael Goldberg
Islamic Studies—Thomas Whitcomb, Ph.D.
Islamic Art—Judith Lerner, Ph.D.
Creative Writing—Paul Bowles, Frederic Tuten, Ph.D.

Join us for a unique summer experience in the beautiful city of Tangier in the kingdom of Morocco overlooking the Straits of Gibraltar. On the 31-acre modern campus of the American School of Tangier, you will live and work with outstanding artists and teachers from the Visual Arts Faculty. All classes in the program will be small, allowing ample time for personalized instruction. Credits are transferable. Attend additional evening programs with special visiting artists and scholars from New York, Europe and Africa. Moroccan craft demonstrations, and performances by international musicians and dancers.

On the weekends explore Tangier, the worldly city where Delacroix, Marquet and Matisse lived and worked. Or join our excursions to the Royal cities of Meknes, Fez and Rabat, or to legendary Casablanca. This may be your ideal solution to summer. A way to continue serious study and artistic exploration with the opportunity to live in an unfamiliar culture.

Living Accommodations: Modern dormitories of the American School of Tangier, open playing fields, student lounges and a full service dining room. The three-week cost includes tuition (total 4½ credits of study) round trip airfare, New York-Tangier, room, full board and weekend excursions. All credits are transferable. Approval of undergraduate or graduate transfer credit for participation in the Visual Arts Summer in Morocco program should be secured in advance from the applicant's department chairperson or college dean and is the responsibility of the applicant.

For further information contact Greg Miller, Office of International Studies.

SCHOOL OF
VISUAL ARTS
209 EAST 23 STREET, NEW YORK, NEW YORK, 10010 (212) 679-7350

PAUL BOWLES:
A WRITING WORKSHOP IN MOROCCO

Spend an extraordinary summer in Tangier Writing.

First Session: July 2-July 23
Second Session: July 23-August 13

Paul Bowles, acclaimed writer of some of the best stories ever written by an American, and long time resident of Tangier, will conduct an intensive writing workshop for serious writers and advanced students on the 31-acre campus of the American School of Tangier. Mr. Bowles will be assisted by Regina Weinreich, New York writer and instructor of creative writing.

Class size will be limited to allow ample time for personalized instruction and criticism. You will be encouraged to pursue your own individual projects, either novels or short stories. Students will be accepted on the basis of submitted manuscripts.

The Kingdom of Morocco is the summer home for the School of Visual Arts. You will be joining a community of artists and writers who during evenings and weekends will participate together in special seminars and trips to Meknes, Fez and Volubilis.

Tangier has an established tradition of inspiring artists: painters such as Matisse, Marquet and Delacroix, writers of the caliber of William Burroughs, Tennessee Williams and Paul Bowles.

Living accommodations: Single rooms in the modern dormitories of the American School of Tangier, open playing fields, student lounges and a full service dining room. A nearby hotel is also available at a supplementary cost.

The three-week cost includes tuition, round trip airfare (New York-Tangier), room, full board and weekend excursions.

For further information contact Bea Mezel at the Office of International Studies, School of Visual Arts, 209 East 23 Street, New York, N.Y. 10010 (212) 679-7350, ext. 314 or 315.

SCHOOL OF
VISUAL ARTS
209 EAST 23RD STREET, NEW YORK, NEW YORK, 10010, (212) 679-7350

(Top) SUMMER PROGRAM POSTER *Creative Director:* Silas H. Rhodes, *Art Director:* Richard Wilde, *Designer:* Alan Giguère, *Photographer:* W.P. Steinmetz/Image Bank
(Bottom) SUMMER PROGRAM POSTER *Creative Director:* Silas H. Rhodes, *Art Director:* Richard Wilde, *Designer:* Alan Giguère, *Photographer:* G. Cserna

Urbino! Urbino! Urbino!

In the Marche region of Italy, not far from Florence and Perugia, is the extraordinary medieval walled city of Urbino, the birthplace of Bramante and Raphael. Majestically built on two hills overlooking the clear and tranquil Italian landscape, Urbino evokes an image of a world shaped and influenced by great art and artists. So it is that the School of Visual Arts has chosen to make its summer home in this beautiful city. The *Istituto Superiore per le Industrie Artistiche* will be the center for our program. The architectural design of the 14th century convent it once was has been retained in all its original beauty. The interiors, recently renovated, are designed to be modern, sophisticated spaces for serious work in the arts. There are large, sunny, fully equipped studios for painting and graphic design, and the newest technology is featured in both printmaking and photography facilities. Our faculty for this summer session is exceptional. Professionals in their fields, with international reputations, they bring to the program a wealth of talent, experience and commitment. You can expect to be involved in an intense and satisfying work experience that promises to stimulate your creative process.

To live in Urbino, even for a few weeks, is to experience the friendly, relaxed and surprising charms of the fabled "la dolce vita." You'll explore the ancient city's steeply angled streets, sip your morning cappuccino on the square and walk the surrounding countryside dotted with sloping plains and lush vineyards. Lunch by the sea in lovely nearby towns like Pesaro, Ancona, Rimini, Ravenna and Fano, none of them very far away. And when you're ready to be more adventuresome, you can travel to Rome and Florence, Venice and Perugia. We can't promise it's going to be easy to come home, but we do know that Visual Arts Summer in Urbino is sure to be an exciting artistic, aesthetic and cultural three weeks. It may be just the change of scene you've needed to see your work with a different perspective, in a fresh new way.

Raphael; *The Three Graces*, 1504-1505; Museum Condé Chantilly, Chantilly, France

SCHOOL OF
Visual Arts
209 EAST 23RD STREET, NEW YORK, N.Y. 10010

SUMMER PROGRAM POSTER *Creative Director:* Silas H. Rhodes, *Art Director:* David Connolly, *Designer:* Merryl Mayer

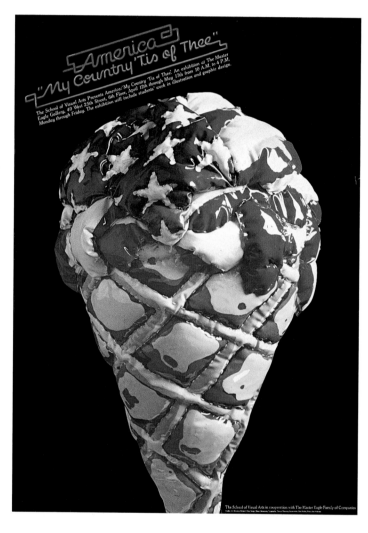

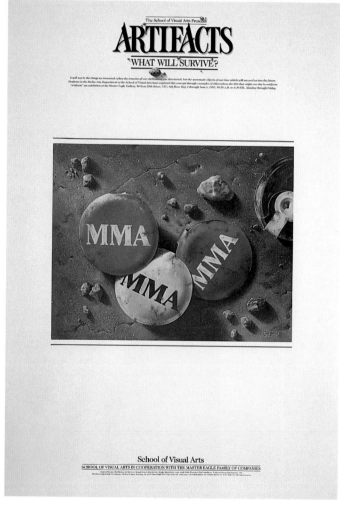

(Left) EXHIBITION POSTER *Art Director:* Richard Wilde, *Designer:* Takao Maysumoto, *Construction:* Chris Bobbin

(Right) EXHIBITION POSTER *Creative Director:* Silas H. Rhodes, *Art Directors:* Richard Wilde and Skip Sorvino, *Illustrator:* Fred Castelluccio

(Left) EXHIBITION POSTER   *Illustrator:* Joseph Ianelli

(Right) EXHIBITION POSTER   *Designer:* Richard Wilde, *Illustrator:* Judi Mintzer

EVE SONNEMAN

" I've done many posters before, but none so specifically about a place. But this time it was perfect because the message was what my work was about. "

Eve Sonneman is a photographer and painter. A member of the faculty at SVA, she teaches third-year Advanced Aesthetics of Photography. A show of large polaroids which she called *Sonnegrams* were exhibited in Paris at La Geode Museum of Science and Technology in 1996. Her fifth book, *How To Touch What*, a collaboration with artist Lawrence Wiener will be published in Paris in 1997, SVA's fiftieth anniversary year.

HOW DID THE IMAGE FOR THIS POSTER COME ABOUT?

I had been doing a whole series of torn and graffitied images around New York City and I had also done a series of similar images in Paris because I was having a big museum show at Beaubourg in 1984. This particular image was included in a group show curated by Diane Waldman for the Visual Arts Museum. And when Silas Rhodes saw the exhibit he wanted to use the image on a poster. At that time, there was a lot of graffiti going on in the subways, and he thought it would be the perfect solution for the poster line. Of course, I was delighted to do it, having taught at Visual Arts for a number of years.

SUBWAY POSTER *Creative Director:* Silas H. Rhodes, *Art Director:* William J. Kobasz, *Designer:* Alan Giguère, *Photographer:* Eve Sonneman, *Copywriter:* Dee Ito

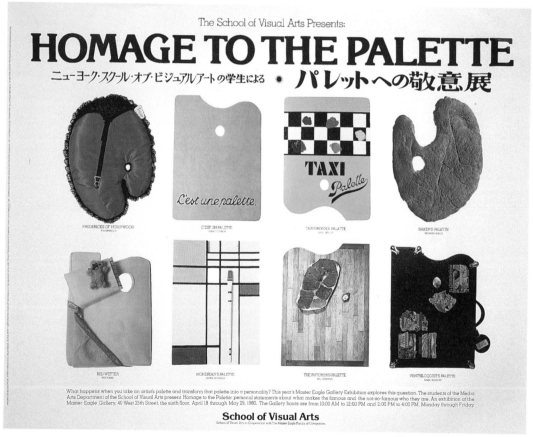

(Top) VISUAL ARTS MUSEUM ANNOUNCEMENT *Creative Director:* Silas H. Rhodes, *Art Director:* William J. Kobasz, *Designer:* Kathi Rota, *Illustrator:* Will Eisner

(Bottom) EXHIBIT ANNOUNCEMENT *Art Director:* Richard Wilde, *Designers:* Diane Addesso/Ayelet Bender

(Top) CATALOG COVER *Creative Director:* Silas H. Rhodes, *Designer:* David Connolly, *Illustrator:* Ron Barbagallo

(Bottom) CATALOG COVER *Creative Director:* Silas H. Rhodes, *Designer:* William J. Kobasz

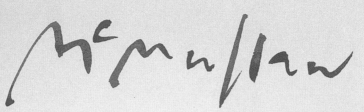

VISUAL ARTS MUSEUM ANNOUNCEMENT *Creative Director:* Silas H. Rhodes, *Designer:* Ayelet Bender, *Illustrator:* James McMullan

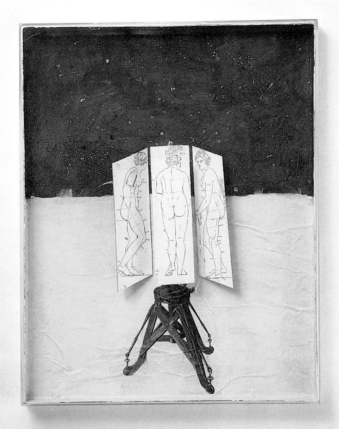

The Dimensional Collage of Robert Weaver

November 5-28, 1988. Curator: Henry Artis. Reception: Saturday November 5, 5-7pm. Visual Arts Museum. 209 East 23 Street, New York City, 10010.

VISUAL ARTS MUSEUM ANNOUNCEMENT *Art Director:* Silas H. Rhodes, *Designer:* Sheri Lee, *Illustrator:* Robert Weaver

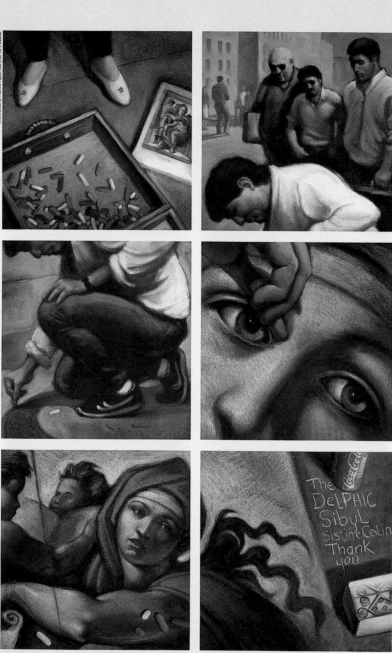

RECRUITMENT POSTER *Creative Director:* Silas H. Rhodes, *Illustrator:* Patrick Pigott

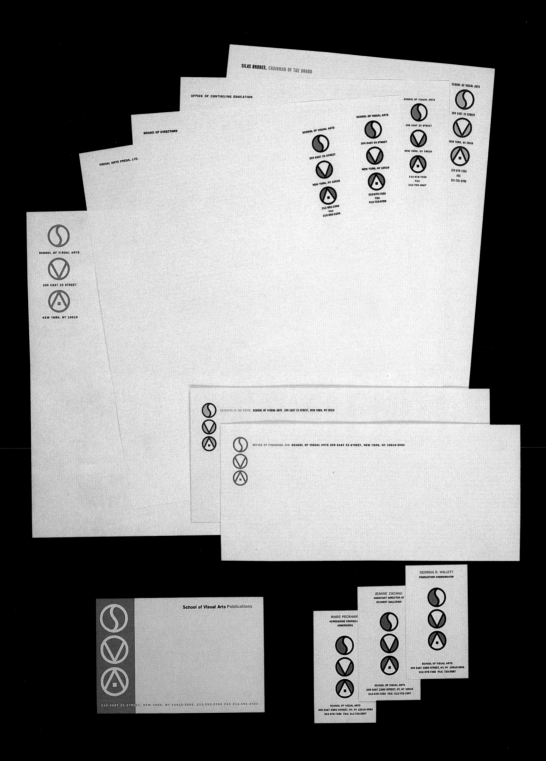

STATIONERY SYSTEM *Creative Director:* Silas H. Rhodes, *Designer:* Paula Scher

SUBWAY POSTER *Creative Director:* Silas H. Rhodes, *Designer:* William J. Kobasz, *Artist:* Laurence M. Gartel

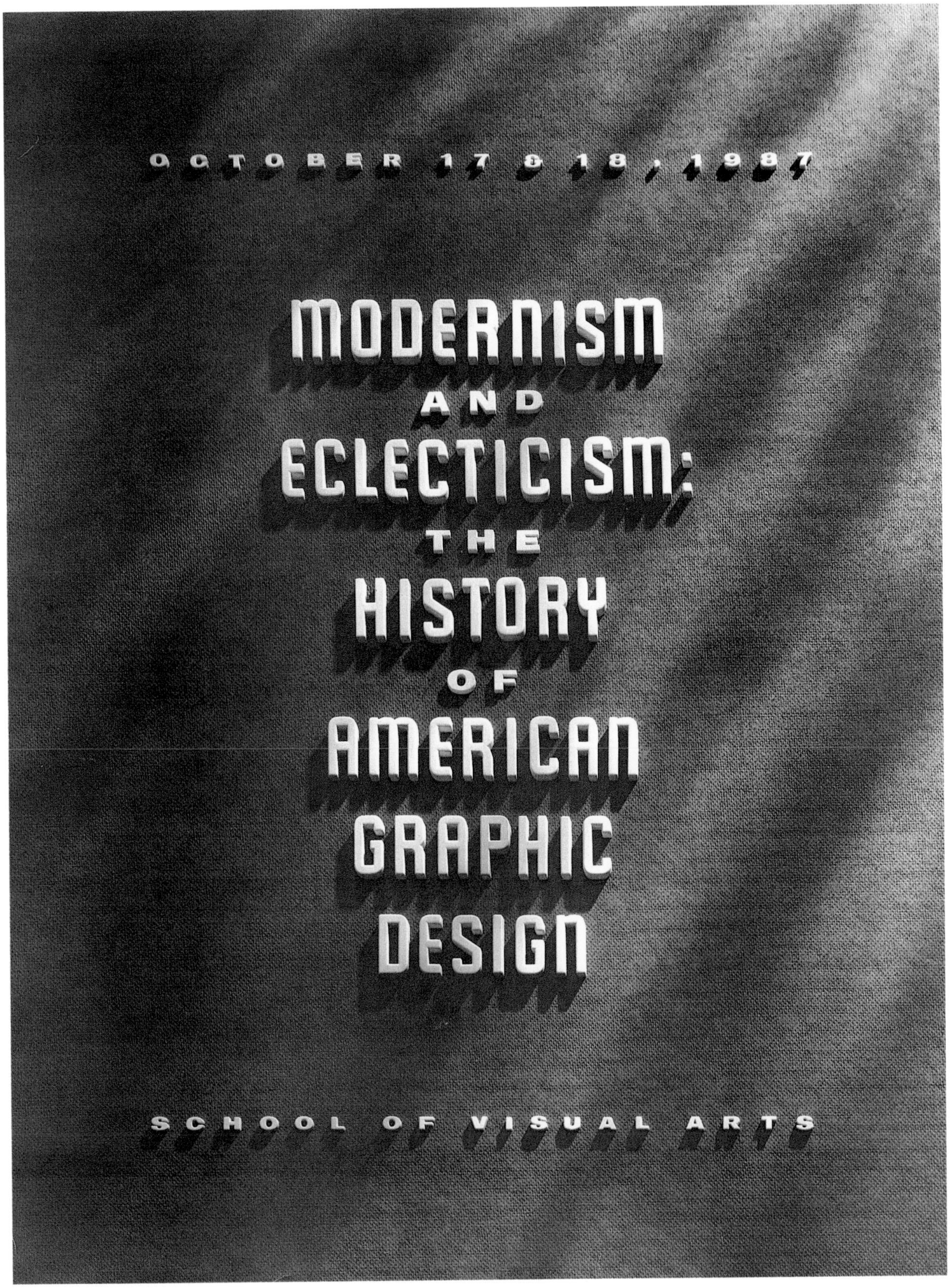

OCTOBER 17 & 18, 1987

MODERNISM
AND
ECLECTICISM:
THE
HISTORY
OF
AMERICAN
GRAPHIC
DESIGN

SCHOOL OF VISUAL ARTS

SYMPOSIUM POSTER *Creative Director:* Silas H. Rhodes, *Designer:* David Connolly, *Photographer:* Chris Varga

School of Visual Arts

SUBWAY POSTER *Creative Director:* Silas H. Rhodes, *Typographer:* David Connolly, *Illustrator:* Marvin Mattelson

RECRUITMENT POSTER *Creative Director:* Silas H. Rhodes, *Designer:* Rosemary Intrieri, *Illustrator:* Jerry Moriarty

THE nineties

the last decade of the 20th Century and the School of Visual Arts turns fifty. Wearing its maturity as it did

its youth, SVA continues its dedication to the idea that change is the only process we can count on. Consequently, students, faculty and staff are continually challenged and the learning environment never remains static. Encouraging and supportive of new approaches to art and creativity, the faculty continues to be drawn from the most innovative professionals working in their individual fields. Beyond that, SVA's legislative activism on all serious arts-related issues facing artists in the nineties is tangible acknowledgement of the value the institution places on the contribution art and artists make to society.

The computer revolution continues and the Internet and World Wide Web are a fact of business, industrial and personal life. SVA's computer graduate program gains an international reputation and its other post-graduate programs are fully enrolled. The Visual Arts Foundation is established as the non-profit arm of the School and its purpose is to further the arts and the cause of artists. In 1993, the institution acquired the Gramercy Women's Residence overlooking historic Gramercy Park and it was converted into dormitory space for its women students.

But the general mood of the country in the nineties is cautious, despite the many social, technological and economic gains in all aspects of society. The collapse of the Soviet Union on the political front and the excesses of the eighties prompted the election of Democrat Bill Clinton as president by a slim margin. Haiti, Northern Ireland, Israel and Bosnia will be factors in the 1996 election. There is an uneasy peace in the world.

The arts have come under severe attack by conservative forces in society who chose to escalate the issue of a controversial exhibit of Robert Mapplethorpe photographs to a national discussion of arts funding resulting in less money for artists. Postmodernist ideas continue to influence the arts, but with a soft art market and no major new art movement on the horizon, artists continue to paint, sculpt, make films and videos as they have always done. In the graphic arts, the influence of computer generated imagery, type and CD-ROM are evident not only in publishing but in advertising, photography and film.

Dramatic changes in the look of the visual landscape are expected in the 21st Century, but it will be the change in the way things are done that will demand re-education—how books, videos, films and photographs are made, how type is set, how portfolios are put together, how people write, read and understand, and how to keep what's unique and personal in artists' work. Institutions like the School of Visual Arts will lead the way with its years of experience and in-depth knowledge of how to teach the nuts and bolts of communication and the art of its times.

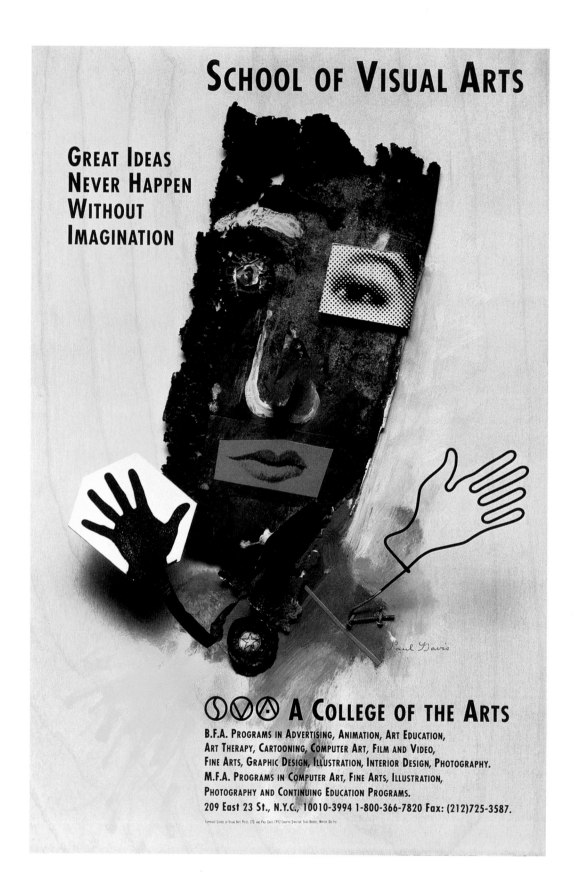

SUBWAY POSTER *Creative Director:* Silas H. Rhodes, *Designer/Illustrator:* Paul Davis, *Copywriter:* Dee Ito

Even a great
idea is only
an idea until you
make it real.

SCHOOL OF VISUAL ARTS

SUBWAY POSTER *Art Director:* Silas H. Rhodes, *Designer:* Rosemary Intrieri, *Illustrator:* Greg Spalenka, *Copywriter:* Dee Ito

SUBWAY POSTER *Creative Director:* Silas H. Rhodes, *Designer/Illustrator:* Tony Palladino

SUBWAY POSTER *Creative Director:* Silas H. Rhodes, *Designer:* Paula Scher, *Copywriter:* Dee Ito

P A U L A   S C H E R

" *I love doing posters, because they're big and people can really see them.*

The best response I had to this poster came from graffiti in the subway.

Someone deliberately got out at five different subway stops in a row and beautifully blacked

out the picture of Churchill and the forefinger, so the poster read: S, F—k, A.

There was no other graffiti on the poster which meant that everyone else respected it

because it was so eloquently done. I actually approve of that. Whenever I design

a subway poster, I like to design it for the graffiti. **"**

Paula Scher began her design career in New York at CBS Records, leaving to form her own company, Koppel & Scher—with Terry Koppel. She is now a partner at Pentagram where her most visible redesign projects have been The New York Public Theater, The Museum of Natural History and *The New York Times Magazine.*

WHAT MOTIVATED YOU TO DESIGN THIS POSTER ON THE COMPUTER?

It was the early nineties, and I thought it would be interesting to stress that the computer was a tool to use to make design. I wanted to design a poster that could only be designed on the computer. On the other hand, I wanted it to reflect the regular design principles that I use when I work without the computer. I began with the notion of making the letters SVA out of individual photographs that become typographic when read a different way from their original intention. Second, I wanted the images to connect somehow or relate back to the line, "Great ideas never happen without imagination." Third, the colors could only happen on the computer. And finally, I used handwriting as a typographic style because I wanted to couple something handmade with something machine made to show that you don't throw away everything personal when you get on the computer.

AND THE ORIGINAL IMAGES, WHERE DID THEY COME FROM?

At first I picked a river to make the S, then I began looking for a road with a curve. I finally found the right one but we still had to do some manipulation to make it read more as an S. Then, the V—Winston Churchill always makes the V for Victory. As for the A—even before doing the poster, I realized that the Eiffel Tower made a perfect A-shape. The image was in the Free-Lance Photo Guild catalog. Lots of people missed that the poster read SVA. Seeing images juxtaposed saying something—even in the graphics community—isn't intuitive.

SUBWAY POSTER *Creative Director:* Silas H. Rhodes, *Designer/Illustrator:* Tony Palladino

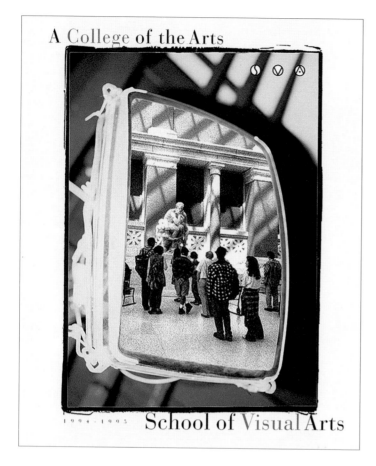

UNDERGRADUATE CATALOG *Creative Director:* Silas H. Rhodes, *Art Director:* Kurt Houser,
Designers: Kurt Houser and Beverley Perkin, *Principal Photographer:* Chris Callis

A Drawing Lesson

The difficulty in drawing from a photograph is knowing what to omit. The photograph contains too much information and generally too many contrary sources of light. Drawing from a photograph is a matter of selection and editing. Degas used photographs in an appropriate way. That is to say, he was not dominated by the material contained in the photo, and felt free to depart from it at will.

Illustration of Matisse sketching a swan at Bois de Bologne

I have often wondered about the distinction between drawing and illustration, and, as usual, the difference is contained within the words themselves. 'Illustration', which comes from the root 'lustrare' means to shed light on, or to make clear. It suggests the idea of a surface of an object interrupting the flow of light. 'Drawing' comes from the root 'trahere', meaning to draw forth, like water from a well or blood from a stone. It suggests the idea of revealing something that is contained within an object and can be drawn out, rather than something that is on the surface. This may explain why those who begin to draw often start with the bones. Both activities require intelligence, perseverance, and talent.

Milton Glaser

Photo of Matisse sketching a swan at the Bois de Bologne

Characteristic bones of the white swan (Cygnus olor)

⊙⊙△ School of Visual Arts

A COLLEGE OF THE ARTS

B.F.A. Programs in Advertising, Animation, Art Education, Art Therapy, Cartooning, Computer Art, Film and Video, Fine Arts, Graphic Design, Illustration, Interior Design, Photography. M.F.A. Programs in Computer Art, Fine Arts, Illustration, Photography and Continuing Education Programs.

209 E. 23 ST., N.Y.C., 10010-3994 1-800-366-7820 FAX: 212-725-3587

"*The School*

was exciting and taught me the

techniques and gave me the understanding

of communication that I still find

successful today."

ROBERT REITZFELD

Partner, Beaver Reitzfeld Advertising, SVA graduate Alumnus of the Year, 1979

MARSHALL ARISMAN

"Creating poster images are among the most interesting assignments I ever get, mainly because I have the opportunity to come up with a visual that will be reproduced the size of a painting. You want it to have impact from a distance and like all good illustration you want it to say something to the viewer quickly. SVA poster assignments are particularly fun to do because living in New York you get to see your work in every subway station and observe people's reactions. You so seldom see people looking at anything you do that you sometimes forget that art really does make connections with an audience outside your family and friends."

Marshall Arisman, illustrator, painter and chairman of the graduate program in illustration at Visual Arts has created several posters for the School in the 30 years he has been on the faculty. His 1995 poster visualized a Cezanne quote, "Art is a harmony parallel to nature."

HOW WAS THIS PARTICULAR POSTER IDEA CONCEIVED?

This was not the usual illustration job. I had been working on a painting of a figure and a turtle in the same frame as part of a series I was doing. It crossed my mind that it might make a strong poster—here was a central image that could read clearly. Then Silas Rhodes told me he needed a new subway poster and emphasized he wanted a representational painting. The quote used as the headline has always been a favorite of mine and for this assignment it worked very well.

YOU'VE DONE POSTERS BEFORE FOR SVA, HOW DO YOU USUALLY WORK?

Well, for some of the other posters, Silas would give me a headline. For example, one of the first posters I did was "Having a talent isn't worth much unless you know what to do with it." Coming up with imagery that works with the words is the illustrator's job, but sometimes I find that good headlines aren't always easy to interpret. In this case, I did a chimp holding a pencil standing on a piece of paper. It's still one of my favorites. Come to think of it, I really like all the things I've done for Visual Arts Press. I think it's because the intent of the art direction is to give the illustrator the opportunity to do his or her best work and there are never any arbitrary limitations.

ART IS A HARMONY PARALLEL TO NATURE. —CÉZANNE

School of Visual Arts

SUBWAY POSTER *Creative Director:* Silas H. Rhodes, *Illustrator:* Marshall Arisman, *Typographer:* Kurt Houser

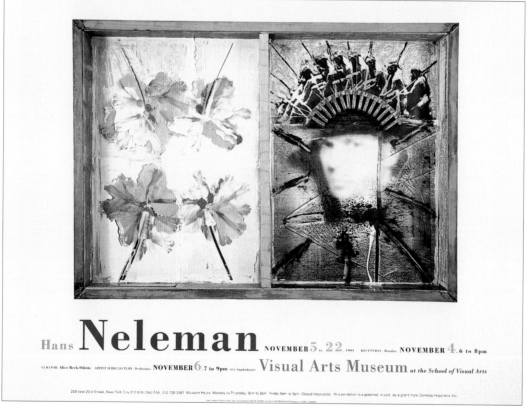

(Top) ANNOUNCEMENT POSTER *Creative Director:* Silas H. Rhodes, *Designer:* Dina Dell'Arciprete
VISUAL ARTS MUSEUM POSTER *Creative Director:* Silas H. Rhodes, *Art Director:* Rosemary Intrieri,
Designer: Laurie Hinzman, *Photography:* Hans Neleman

EXHIBITION POSTER *Creative Director:* Silas H. Rhodes, *Art Director:* Kurt Houser, *Designer:* Johnny Vitorovich, *Illustrator:* Sean Beavers

CATALOG COVER *Creative Director:* Silas H. Rhodes, *Designer:* Kurt Houser, *Illustrator:* Jack Endewelt

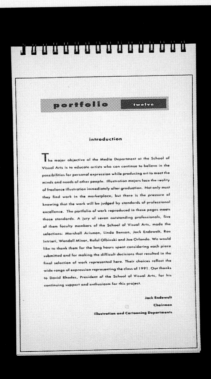

ILLUSTRATION PORTFOLIOS (Top) *Illustrator:* Matthew Rotunda (Bottom from Left) *Illustrator:* Philippe Lardy,
Designer: Laurie Hinzman, *Illustrator:* Tristan Elwell

Words

In words as fashions the same rule will hold,
Alike fantastic if too new or old.
Be not the first by whom the new are tried,
Nor yet the last to lay the old aside.

Alexander Pope

Image

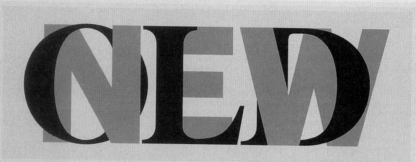

Thoughts

This poem is impossible. Silas usually has a better touch with his choice of quotations. This one generates no imagery at all. Maybe the words can make the image without anything else happening. What's the heart of this poem? Don't be trendy if you want to be serious. Isn't doing the poster this way trendy in itself? I guess one could reduce the idea further by suggesting that the new emerges behind and through the old, like this:

Not bad, but more didactic than visual. Maybe what wants to be said is that the old and the new are locked in a dialectical embrace—a kind of dance where each defines the other.

Am I being simple-minded? Is it the kind of simple that looks obvious or the kind that looks profound? There is a significant difference. This could be embarrassing. Actually, I realize fear of embarrassment drives me as much as any other ambition.

Do you think this sort of thing could really attract a student to the school?

Milton Glaser

School of Visual Arts

A COLLEGE OF THE ARTS

B.F.A. Programs in Advertising, Animation, Art Education, Art Therapy, Cartooning, Computer Art, Film and Video, Fine Arts, Graphic Design, Illustration, Interior Design, Photography. M.F.A. Programs in Computer Art, Fine Arts, Illustration, Photography and Continuing Education Programs.

209 E. 23 ST., N.Y.C., 10010-3994 1-800-366-7820 FAX: 212-725-3587

SUBWAY POSTER *Creative Director:* Silas H. Rhodes, *Designer:* Milton Glaser

SUBWAY POSTER *Creative Director:* Silas H. Rhodes, *Illustrator:* Jerry Moriarty, *Typographer:* Nancy Mazzei

Congratulations, School of VISUAL ARTS! Turning 50 is an occasion for great celebration. Our modest beginnings could not have predicted our dramatic growth, becoming the largest independent art college in the United States. But we are most proud of graduating outstanding students who have benefited from working with a select faculty of professionals who teach because they want to. Today, we believe that our commitment to enlarging our students' art vocabulary to include ground-breaking technological tools will not only change the way art is produced but will influence art itself in the next millennium.

SUBWAY POSTER *Creative Director:* Silas H. Rhodes, *Designer:* George Tscherny, *Photograher:* Oscar Villegas

CORPORATE IDENTITY *Designer:* George Tscherny

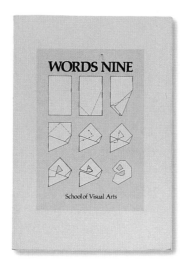

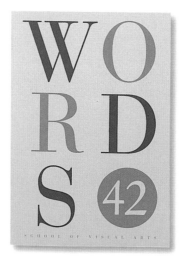

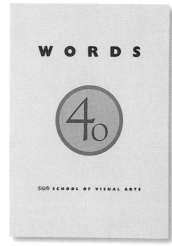

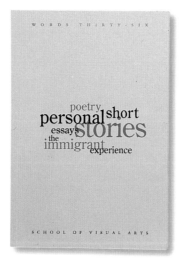

WORDS BOOK COVERS (Clockwise from Top Left) *Designers:* Sue A. Taube, Kurt Houser,
Michael Choo, Cynthia Jacquette, Kurt Houser, Cynthia Jacquette

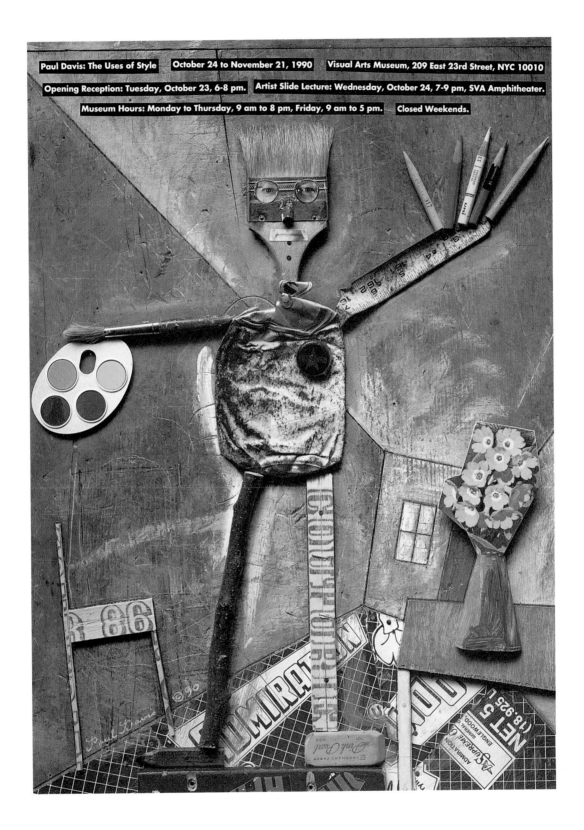

VISUAL ARTS MUSEUM EXHIBITION POSTER *Illustrator/Designer:* Paul Davis

yugo next

There are many things created with the expectation of excellence. However, few live up to that dream. Is it a case of wasted potential or a lack of ingenuity? The YUGO is one such creation. As an automobile it was ultimately a failure, but the collective imagination of 25 artists have reconsidered the use of the Yugoslavian automobile. The result is "YUGO NEXT," an exhibition initially held at Grand Central Station, now touring the world.

(Top) *Artist:* Robert Johnston (Center) *Artist:* James Diresta (Bottom) *Artist:* Celia Landegger

THE
masters
SERIES

In 1988 SVA launched a new project: The Masters Series—to select distinguished artists who have created a significant body of work within the field of communication and design. The honoree is invited to hold a comprehensive, retrospective exhibition in the Visual Arts Museum. The following artists are Masters Series honorees since 1988:

Paul Rand, October 1988

Milton Glaser, October 1989

Massimo Vignelli, February/March 1991

Lou Dorfsman, October 1991

George Tscherny, October 1992

George Lois, October 1994

Deborah Sussman, March/April 1995

Ivan Chermayeff, October 1995

Saul Bass, March/April 1996

Mary Ellen Mark, October 1996

Seymour Chwast, October 1997 (to be shown)

(Top) *Artist:* Paul Rand   (Bottom) *Artist:* Milton Glaser

In the new computer age the proliferation of typefaces and type manipulations represents a new level of visual pollution threatening our culture. Out of thousands of typefaces, all we need are a few basic ones, and trash the rest. So come and see

A Few Basic Typefaces

The Masters Series: Massimo Vignelli
February 22 to March 8, 1991

Reception: Thursday, February 21, 6 to 8 pm
Lecture: Tuesday, February 26, 7 to 9 pm,
School of Visual Arts Amphitheater.

The third in a series of exhibitions honoring the great visual communicators of our time.

Visual Arts Museum, 209 East 23rd Street, NYC, 10010
Museum Hours: Monday to Thursday, 9 am to 8 pm,
Friday, 9 am to 5 pm. Closed Weekends.

The Masters Series is supported in part by a grant from the Architecture, Planning and Design program of the New York State Council on the Arts. ©1991 by the Visual Arts Press, LTD.

Artist: Massimo Vignelli

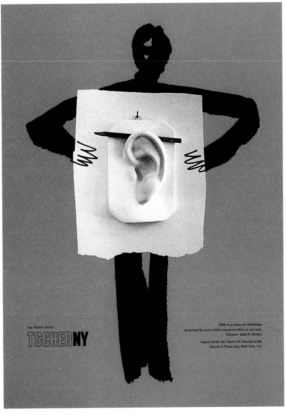

(Top) *Artist:* Lou Dorfsman   (Bottom) *Artist:* George Tscherny

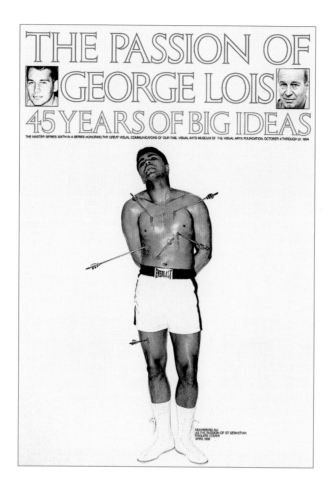

(Top) *Artist:* George Lois   (Bottom) *Artist:* Deborah Sussman

The Master Series: Ivan Chermayeff Graphic Design: Art & Process
Eighth in the series, Exhibition: October 2nd to October 20th 1995
Lecture: Thursday, October 5th, 7 pm. Museum Hours:
Monday–Thursday 9 am–8pm, Friday 9 am–5pm.
Visual Arts Museum at the School of Visual Arts
209 East 23rd Street, New York, New York 10010

(Top) *Artist:* Ivan Chermayeff (Bottom) *Artist:* Saul Bass

"art is..."

For one of the events celebrating our 50th year, ten artists from the faculty were selected to respond to "Art is..." by creating posters for subway platforms and bus shelters which inform the community that the conventional wisdom about what art is is not what Art is... .

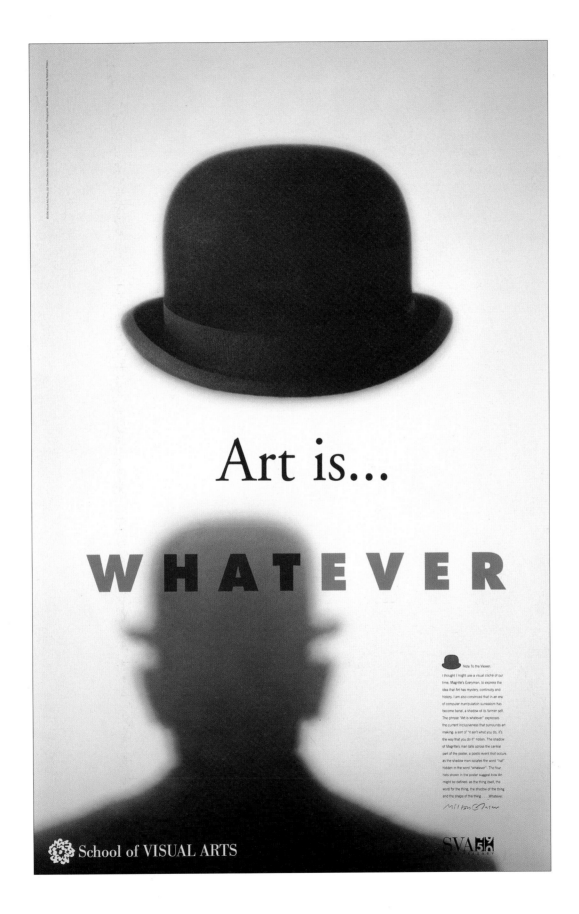

SUBWAY POSTER *Creative Director:* Silas H. Rhodes, *Designer:* Milton Glaser, *Photographer:* Matthew Klein

SUBWAY POSTER *Creative Director:* Silas H. Rhodes, *Designer/Illustrator:* Paul Davis

SUBWAY POSTER *Creative Director:* Silas H. Rhodes, *Designer:* Paula Scher

SUBWAY POSTER *Creative Director:* Silas H. Rhodes, *Painting:* Jerry Moriarty, *Typographer:* Kurt Houser

SUBWAY POSTER *Creative Director:* Silas H. Rhodes, *Artist:* Gil Ashby, *Typographer:* Kurt Houser

SUBWAY POSTER *Creative Director:* Silas H. Rhodes, *Collage and Painting:* Marshall Arisman, *Typographer:* Kurt Houser

SUBWAY POSTER *Creative Director:* Silas H. Rhodes, *Illustrator/Designer:* James McMullan

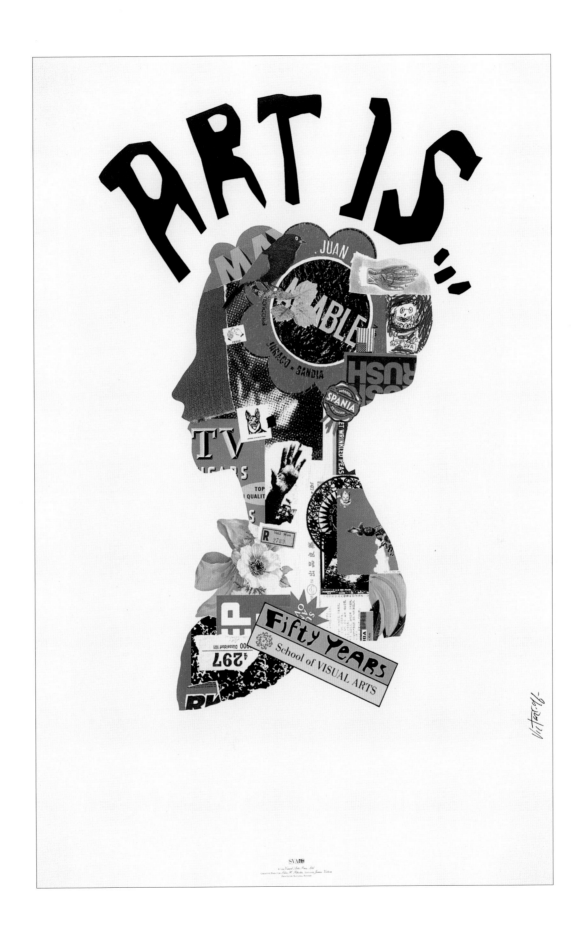

SUBWAY POSTER *Creative Director:* Silas H. Rhodes, *Artist:* Eve Sonneman, *Typographer:* Kurt Houser

of late, the respect with which the public has viewed higher education has been diminished. This change in perception is caused chiefly by the belief that colleges and universities show an increasing distance between what they say and what, in fact, they do. Claims of excellence are easily offered but are not readily apparent. Calls of conscience are compromised by budgetary considerations and the fear of appearances. Disinterested conduct is difficult to find.

In the smaller world of art education, faculty of art colleges and departments are lauded for their professionalism, their empathy and their instructional prowess. In most instances, their work is not in the public eye, their consultation arrangements are hidden from view, and there is no way to truly evaluate their teaching.

The work published on the preceding pages is an indication that in the past fifty years, Visual Arts has insisted that the work of its faculty be on public display so that the professionalism of the faculty can be readily judged. In short, it is one of the many attempts to close the gap between word and deed.

As we approach the next millennium, history has shown us that we will be inundated by predictions which purport to tell us about the future. Many, touting new technologies, will be overly optimistic, others will be overly pessimistic—almost apocalyptic. None will be correct.

The shape and texture of the world of the twenty-first century is not yet clear. Claims to know with precision how to educate artists for this future are suspect. Therefore, the challenges for the next fifty years in arts education will be met by an institution which is flexible enough to accommodate rapid changes, while at the same time adhering to a small set of principles which will influence all of what the institution does.

The challenge, therefore, is to continue to apply the principles of excellence and professionalism to the new problems which will confront us in the next millennium. We believe Visual Arts is ready for this challenge.

D A V I D   R H O D E S

December, 1996

biographies

Marshall Arisman

Education: B.F.A., Pratt Institute

Occupation: Illustrator; Fine Artist; Chair, Master of Fine Arts Degree Program in Illustration as Visual Essay, SVA

Books include: *Frozen Images, Art of the Times, Artists' Christmas Cards, Images of Labor, Fitcher's Bird*

Publications include: *The New York Times, Urban Journal, Politiks, The Nation, Esquire, Playboy, Sports Illustrated, Time, Rolling Stone, Penthouse, Mother Jones, The Boston Globe.* Articles About the Artist in: *Graphis; Idea; Omni; Illustration, Tokyo; CA; Creative Review,* London

One-Person Exhibitions include: York Gallery; Corridor Gallery; Sindin Galleries; Kamikaze; Visual Arts Museum; travelling exhibition, Images of Labor, District 1199, NY; Smithsonian Institution; Galerie Philippe Guimiot, Belgium; Harcourts Gallery; Parco Galleries, Tokyo

Collections include: Smithsonian Institution, Brooklyn Museum

Awards include: Ida Jaskill Award; Playboy Illustrator of the Year Award; Gold Medal, Society of Publication Designers; Silver Medal, Society of Illustrators; AIGA; *Graphis Annual,* Graphis Poster Awards; *CA Annual;* Art Directors Club; *Print Casebook*

Paul Davis

Education: School of Visual Arts

Occupation: Illustrator; Graphic Designer; Principal, Paul Davis Studio; Faculty, SVA

Exhibitions include: Museum of Modern Art, Kamakura, Kyoto and Gumma, Japan; Centre Georges Pompidou, Paris

Books include: *Paul Davis Posters and Paintings, Paul Davis Faces, The Arcadia Seasonal Cookbook*

Clients include: American Express, CBS Records, Condé Nast, The "21" Club, Warner Books, The United Nations, Harper & Row, Olivetti, Time Inc., Museum of Modern Art, The Kennedy Center, Simon & Schuster

Awards include: Lifetime Achievement Medal, AIGA; Gold and Silver Medals, Art Directors Club; Silver Medal, Society of Publication Designers; Silver Medal, Primera Bienal de Artes Graficas, Columbia; Bronze Medal, VIII Poster Biennale, Poland; Drama Desk Award

Sal DeVito

Education: A.A., SUNY Farmingdale, School of Visual Arts

Occupation: Creative Director, DeVito Verdi; Faculty, SVA; Formerly, Vice President, Associate Creative Director, Levine, Huntley, Schmidt & Beaver, Inc.

Awards include: Gold Medal, The One Show; Gold and Silver Lion, Cannes Film Festival; ANDY; Art Directors Club; CLIO

Milton Glaser

Education: Cooper Union; Academy of Fine Arts, Bologna, Italy

Occupation: President and Creative Director, Milton Glaser, Inc.; Board Member, Faculty, SVA; Trustee, Cooper Union; Formerly, Co-Founder and President, Push Pin Studios; Co-Founder, President and Creative Director, *New York;* Vice President and Co-Chair, AIGA; President, International Design Conference, Aspen, CO

One-Person Exhibitions include: Museum of Modern Art; European traveling exhibition - Barcelona, Venice, Bologna, and Centre Georges Pompidou, Paris

Clients include: Electra Records, Grand Union, Queens College, Alessi, World Trade Center, The Rainbow Room, Lincoln Center, World Health Organization, Carnegie Hall, Julliard School

Awards include: Fulbright Scholarship; Hall of Fame, Art Directors Club; Honorary Fellow, Society of Arts, England; Gold Medal, Society of Illustrators; Saint Gaudens Medal, Cooper Union. Honorary Doctorates: Minneapolis Institute of Fine Art, Moore College of Art, Philadelphia Museum School, School of Visual Arts

Books Illustrated include: *Gogol, The Works of Appolinaire, J'Irai Cracher Sur Vos Tombes, The Illustrated Don Juan, Rimes de la Mere Oie, Fish in the Sky, Cats and Bats and Things with Wings, The Smallest Elephant in the World*

Phil Hays

Education: Kansas City Art Institute; Ringling School of Art and Design; Art Center College of Design, CA

Occupation: Chairman, Illustration Department, Art Center College of Design, CA

Clients include: Avco-Lycoming, Coca-Cola, American Airlines, Alitalia, Columbia Records, Motown Records, EMI America, Elektra Asylum, Blue Note

Publications include: *Graphis, Esquire, New York, Playboy, The New York Times*

Exhibitions include: D'Arcy Gallery; New York Historical Society; U.S. State Department Exhibition; Cooper-Hewitt Museum; Mead Art Museum, Amherst, MA; University of South Florida

Collections include: Museum of Modern Art; The Metropolitan Museum of Art; Smithsonian Institution

Awards include: Gold and Silver medals, Society of Illustrators; Gold and Silver medals, Art Directors Club; over 200 Awards of Excellence, Society of Illustrators, Art Directors Club, AIGA

Marvin Mattelson

Education: B.F.A., Philadelphia College of Art

Occupation: Illustrator; Faculty, SVA

Publications include: *Step-by-Step Graphics, Graphis Annual, Illustrators Annual, CA Annual, Idea, Print, Art Direction*

Clients include: *Scientific American; Penthouse; Playboy; The Atlantic;* Dell; Bantam; Viking-Penguin; CBS Records; Westinghouse; Fuji; Cutty Sark; Hennessey; E.F. Hutton; Union Carbide; NYNEX; Bronx Zoo; Lincoln Mercury; *Esquire, New York; The New York Times; National Lampoon; Saturday Review;* Young & Rubicam; McCann-Erickson; Doyle, Dane, Bernbach; Benton & Bowles; Wells, Rich, Greene, Inc.;

Time; Newsweek; IBM; AT&T; A&E Network; CBS; The Hartford; Met Life; *Life*; Geffen Films

Exhibition: Society of Illustrators

Awards include: Society of Illustrators, AIGA, Art Directors Club, Society of Publication Designers, ANDY, Desi, *CA*

James McMullan

Education: Pratt Institute

Occupation: Owner, President, James McMullan, Inc.; Illustrator; Faculty, SVA; Formerly, Push Pin Studios; Director and Vice President, AIGA

Exhibitions include: Southampton College; 10th International Poster Biennial; Grand Palais, Paris; Lowell Gallery; Giraffics Gallery; Headley-Whitney Museum; Margo Feiden Galleries

Clients include: *New York, Rolling Stone,* CUNY, *Time, Sports Illustrated, The New Yorker,* Lincoln Center Theater

Books include: *Drawing From Life, The Noisy Giants Tea Party, Revealing Illustrations, Particularly Cats and Rufus, Nutcracker Noel*

Publications include: *Idea, Graphis, Print, The Art of the Broadway Poster, The Art of New York, Innovators of American Illustration*

Awards: Gold and Silver Medals, Hamilton King Award, Society of Illustrators; ANDY; Drama Desk Award

Jerry Moriarty

Education: B.F.A., Pratt Institute

Occupation: Illustrator, Painter; Faculty, SVA

One-Person Exhibitions include: Corridor Gallery, Kamikaze, Printed Matter

Group Exhibitions include: University of Massachusetts; Institute of Contemporary Arts, London; Blue Coat Gallery, Liverpool; Lambiek Gallery, Amsterdam

Publications include: *Seventeen, Esquire, Eros, Sports Illustrated,* Time-Life, *Denver Post.* Children's books for: Young Scott; Scholastic Books

Contributor: *Raw, Picture Story, El Vibora*

Author/Illustrator: *Jack Survives*

Awards include: National Endowment for the Arts, Society of Illustrators

Tony Palladino

Education: Studied with Mark Rothko, William Baziotes, Robert Motherwell

Occupation: Graphic Designer, Advertising Art Director, Marketing Consultant; Faculty, SVA

Clients include: Mobil Oil; Backer Spielvogel Bates, Inc.; Wells, Rich, Greene, Inc.; Ally Gargano; New York Philharmonic; Phoenix House

Books include: *Once There Was a General, ABC Bedtime Stories*

Exhibitions include: Visual Arts Museum, Museum of Modern Art, Litchfield Library, Elizabeth Weiner Gallery

Collections include: Museum of Modern Art; Ohio Museum; Republic of San Marino Museum, Italy; Mobil Oil; Prudential Life Insurance Company; Chesebrough-Ponds, Inc.

Awards include: Hall of Fame, Art Directors Club; Type Directors Club; Art Directors Club, New Jersey and London; Magazine & Publishers Show; Edgar Allen Poe Award

Eve Sonneman

Education: B.F.A., University of Illinois; M.A., University of New Mexico

Occupation: Fine Art Photographer, Author; Faculty, SVA

Represented by: Zabriskie Gallery, Paris; Cirrus Gallery, Los Angeles

One-Person Exhibitions include: Queens Museum; Zabriskie Gallery, Paris; Museum of Modern Art, Costa Rica; Centre Georges Pompidou, Paris

Group Exhibitions: Biennale of Sydney, Australia; Venice Biennale; Paris Biennale; Documenta VI; The Metropolitan Museum of Art; Museum of Modern Art; Hudson River Museum; Castelli Gallery; Cartier Foundation Show, France; Zabriskie Gallery

Film Screenings include: Ann Arbor Film Festival, Art Institute of Chicago, Whitney Museum Art Resources Center, Gallery Farideh Cadot, Rheinisches Landesmuseum, New York Cable TV

Collections: Museum of Modern Art; The Metropolitan Museum of Art; National Gallery of Australia, Canberra; Centre Georges Pompidou, Paris; Menil Foundation, Houston, TX; Toppan Museum, Japan; Art Institute of Chicago

Books include: *Counterparts, Mirrors and Windows, Real Time, Roses are Read, Americas Cottage Gardens, Where Birds Live*

Reviews in: *Life, Artforum, Art in America, Flash Art, The New York Times, Newsweek, Modern Photography, The New Yorker, ARTnews, Mademoiselle, Arts, Art Direction, Le Figaro, Elle Decor, The Wall Street Journal*

Awards include: Cartier Award, France; Polaroid Corporation Grant in the Arts; National Endowment for the Arts

Paula Scher

Education: B.F.A., Tyler School of Art

Occupation: Partner, Pentagram; Faculty, SVA; Formerly, Senior Art Director, CBS Records; Gips & Balkind Associates; Board of Directors, AIGA

Clients include: Manhattan/Blue Note Records, European *Travel & Leisure,* Swatch Watch U.S.A., Champion International Corp.

Publications include: *Print, ADWEEK, AIGA Journal, Graphis, Graphis Annual, Idea* (Japan), *Industrial Design, AIGA Annual, Art Directors Club Annual, Novum Gebrauchsgraphik*

Author/Designer: *The Honeymoon Book, The Brownstone*

Collections include: Museum of Modern Art; Library of Congress; Centre Georges Pompidou, Paris; Maryland Institute of Art; Chicago Institute of Art

Awards include: Gold Medal, Art Directors Club; Gold Medal, Society of Illustrators; AIGA; *CA; Art Direction;* Type Directors Club; ANDY

George Tscherny

Education: Newark School of Fine and Industrial Art, Pratt Institute

Occupation: Graphic Designer; Formerly, Design Consultant, The Ford Foundation; President, AIGA

Clients have included: Air Canada, American Can Company, Bankers Trust Co., Burlington Industries, Champion Papers, CPC International, General Dynamics, Goethe House, IBM, Johnson & Johnson, Mobil, Pan AM, SEI Corporation

One-Man Retrospective: Visual Arts Museum

Corporate Identity Projects include: W.R. Grace & Co., Texasgulf Co.

Books include: *A History of Graphic Design, Contemporary Designers, Visual Puns in Design, Thirty Centuries of Graphic Design, Who's Who in Graphic Art, Who's Who in America, Who's Who in Graphic Design, The 100 Best Posters from Europe and the United States, Expressive Typography*

Publications include: *American Artist, Novum Gebrauchsgraphik, Folio 4, Print, Graphis, CA.*

Collections include: Museum of Modern Art; The Cooper-Hewitt Museum; Kunstgewerbemuseum, Zurich

Awards include: Commemorative postage stamp design, United States Postal Service; Gold Medal, AIGA

index

photographers

copywriters

credits

Creative Director: Silas H. Rhodes

Editor: PBC International, Inc.

Writer: Dee Ito

Art Director/Designer: Kurt Houser